Progress
through
Separate
Development

SOUTH AFRICA IN PEACEFUL TRANSITION

*An aerial view of central Johannesburg—the most modern
city in Africa and the home of more than one million people.
Johannesburg is typical of the areas of South Africa which
were settled by the white man.*

Contents

*This book was compiled and issued by the New York office
of the South African Department of Information in 1967.*

Introduction

AMERICANS have traditionally prided themselves on their ability to look at all sides of a question before passing final judgment. The question of South Africa has many sides – not only racial – that are little known and appreciated in the outside world.

The question of the relationships between various population groups is in the spotlight of world attention today. The Republic of South Africa has had more than its share of this attention because history has left it a legacy of complex population problems.

No dynamic policy dealing with that most unpredictable of God's creations—man—can ever be crystallized into a few trite phrases. In South Africa, with its multi-national population, the policy of Separate Development has been evolved in an endeavour to find a satisfactory pattern for the harmonious co-existence of divergent national communities within the same present geopolitical borders.

Those people in the South African Government who are closely connected with, or formulate, the policies underlying this development are the ones who are best suited to present them. This book is a compilation of the views expressed publicly by the members of the South African Government.

The population of South Africa is composed of:

The White Nation	3,500,200

THE BANTU NATIONS:

Xhosas	3,324,501
Zulus	3,167,177
Swazis	334,310
Ndebele	294,253
North Sotho	1,233,087
South Sotho	132,844
Tswana	1,324,977
Tsonga	511,093
Venda	245,829

OTHER GROUPS:

Coloureds	1,648,000
Asians	600,000

Mr. John Vorster, Prime Minister of the Republic of South Africa. Mr. Vorster is leader of the governing National Party.

"I believe in the policy of separate development, not only as a philosophy but also as the only practical solution in the interest of everyone to eliminate frictions, and to do justice to every population group as well as every individual.

"I say to the Coloured people, as well as to the Indians and the Bantu that the policy of separate development is not a policy which rests upon jealousy, fear or hatred. It is not a denial of the human dignity of anyone nor is it so intended. On the contrary, it gives the opportunity to every individual within his own sphere, not only to be a man or woman in every sense, but it also creates the opportunity for them to develop and advance without restriction or frustration as circumstances justify, and in accordance with the demands of developments achieved.

"My appeal therefore to every leader of every population group is this: the best of service to humanity lies in service to one's own people. Every population group has what is its own, which is beautiful and which can be developed.

"There is more work for every leader among his own people than he can do in his lifetime. I believe that we, the Whites, the Coloureds, the Indians and the Bantu, will show the world that we do not only have in principle the answer to the race question but that we will also prove it in practice.

"I am aware that we are a small country and that our population is small. But the greatness of a people does not lie in its numbers but in the character, the drive, the ability to work, the self-respect and the faith of its people."

6

Chapter I

South Africa's Problem

"*The essential condition (to a stable and prosperous country) is that racial domination will have to be removed. As long as domination of one race by another exists there will be resistance and unrest. Consequently, the solution should be sought by means of a policy which is calculated to eliminate domination in every form and in every respect.*" Dr. H. F. Verwoerd, former Premier, speaking in the South African Parliament.

ON THE THRESHOLD OF TOMORROW...

SOUTH Africa's problem is unique. Nowhere in the world, and never in history, has a situation developed which is quite similar. The solution must, therefore, also be unique. And yet everybody, everywhere, whether knowledgeable or quite uninformed, would like to impose theoretical ideas and principles or solutions found to be, or thought to be, useful elsewhere, on this different situation."

8

An aerial view of the Cape Peninsula showing the city of Cape Town nestling under Table Mountain. The first white settlers landed here in 1652 when the Dutch East India Company opened a refreshment station at what was to become the modern city seen in the picture (left) .

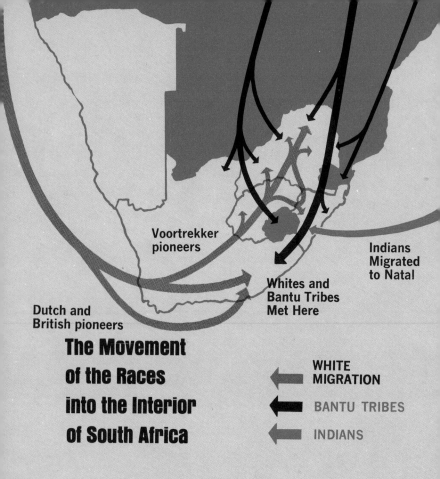

Voortrekker
pioneers

Indians
Migrated
to Natal

Whites and
Bantu Tribes
Met Here

Dutch and
British pioneers

The Movement
of the Races
into the Interior
of South Africa

WHITE
MIGRATION

BANTU TRIBES

INDIANS

The first permanent settlers from Europe came to the Cape of
Good Hope in 1652 when Jan Van Riebeeck established a supply
station to provide fresh food and vegetables for merchantmen of
the Dutch East India Company trading with the East. Sporadic immigration from Western Europe made Cape Town a thriving outpost,
and the farmers began pushing inland. They moved into what is
now the Eastern Cape Province, where by the mid-eighteenth century
they encountered the vanguard of the Bantu tribes who had been
moving south. Insecurity on the border and dissatisfaction with
British rule forced Voortrekker pioneers to trek northward into the
interior and eastward into the vacuum created by the Zulu tyrant
Shaka's wars of extermination in Natal. At the time of Van Riebeeck's
landing, masses of Bantu were slowly approaching from the North,
from the Lake regions of Central Africa. These Bantu tribes settled
along the Eastern seaboard, in the valleys of the Drakensberg and
on the warm, fertile plains on the seaward slopes of the mountains.

Historical Encounter in Vacant Land

More than 300 years ago two population groups, equally foreign to South Africa, converged in rather small numbers on what was practically an empty country. Neither group colonized the other's country or robbed him by invasion and oppression. Each settled and gradually extended his settlements, and in the main each sought a different part in which to dwell. There were clashes and frontier wars, and border areas were conquered, but since then the white man has added, and is adding, more land to the Bantu areas from that portion which he himself settled and intended to be his own.

No Colonialism

The first point is, therefore, that there was no colonialism, only separate settlement by each group, nearly simultaneously, and each had the chance for more than 300 years to develop his country to serve his growing population group. In fact only in South Africa did the white man deliberately reserve land for the Bantu and endeavoured (mostly in vain) to train him to make the best use of it, as he did with his own, and to such good purpose that the black man came to him for employment, food and the good things of life. The white man, therefore, has not only an undoubted stake in, and right to, the land which he developed into a modern industrial state from denuded plains and empty valleys and isolated mountains, but according to all principles of morality it was his, is his and must remain his.

It is true that, in the course of time, he received within his country growing numbers of black people. Some fled to him for protection, driven out of their own country by internecine strife and the heavy hand of tyrants. Many came to him seeking relief from hunger or attracted by the bright lights of cities or by the desire for money and the good things of life.

Character of the Nation

It is also true that elsewhere immigrants from one country to another could become fully-fledged citizens with political rights under certain conditions. It must, however, not be forgotten that for that very reason such countries could, and did, and do, ration and restrict entrance to numbers which would not change the character of the nation or the control of its country, its culture and ideals or its very existence.

South Africa did not need to exercise this control and

The Union Buildings, Pretoria, administrative seat of the government of the Republic of South Africa.

could be very liberal in giving entry, providing aid and a better life to all who entered, even illegally, because such consequences did not come into the picture on the South African scene.

The non-Whites who entered the white man's country, or the urban areas, came solely to seek employment, safety, health, education—all of which was provided freely by the white man.

No Desire to Take Political Power

There was thus no question of robbing the white man of his country by any political result of this entry in huge numbers, or by the natural increase of his population under the white man's protection and care.

In fact, it seemed then that for all time the Whites would, as guardians, even have to rule the black man's country as part of their own (in his interest) because he could not be developed to do this properly for himself. The white man therefore allowed the influx to continue until he was outnumbered four to one, and even now, against his will, streams of illegal black immigrants flow across his borders from many parts of Africa because of the better wages and way of life they find in this land of so-called oppression.

Justice for White and Black

What is the solution to this dilemma which history and the unexpected awakening of the black man has handed us? Theorists and others who, far away, can remain unaffected themselves, but philosophize gladly on the handing over of what is the possession of others, expect the white South

The Legislative Assembly of the Transkei meets here in the new state's capital, Umtata. The Legislative Assembly (left), which was popularly known as the Bunga, has been the hub of constitutional development in the Transkei since the late 1920's. In 1956 the district councils of the Transkei were fully integrated when the Transkei's Territorial Authority was established. In 1961 this Territorial Authority approached the South African Government with the request for self-rule and in 1962 a committee of Transkei leaders deliberated among themselves and later with the Republican Government in drawing up the constitution for the new state. In November, 1963 the first elections were held.

The city of Durban has the largest harbour and handles the most goods on the whole African continent.

South Africa is a veritable mineral treasure house. Here copper ingots are being loaded in Cape Town harbour.

African to give way gradually (and knowing that after the first step the pace will become uncontrollable) his country and his possessions and, indeed, ultimately his whole nationhood and existence.

Justice is Indivisible

Where does morality come in if this is demanded? If there must be justice for the black man, there must be justice for the white man and the Coloured, too, who will both be affected and suppressed.

Cannot you understand us fighting to the death for our existence? And yet we do not only seek and fight for a solution which will mean our survival, but seek one which will grant survival and full development, politically and economically, to each of the other national groups as well, and we are even prepared to pay a high price out of our earnings for their future.

The moral problem, just like the political problem, is to find a way out of this extremely difficult and complicated situation, caused by the fact that no longer, as in the past, is the black man incapable or undesirous of participation in the control of his political destinies. Nor is there any longer anyone prepared to oppress him by refusing the fulfilment of such ambitions in a form fair to all. What is the solution?

Elsewhere in Africa

In certain parts of Africa where the white man also ruled alone before, a solution is relatively easy. Those who find it easy there and do not realise the great difference between the two situations, are unfortunately tempted to wish to transplant that solution to South Africa. We refer to the countries of Africa which undoubtedly belong to the black man by settlement and inheritance, although they were taken over, administered and developed by different white nations. It is right that their land should now politically become their own.

Then there are in Africa other states where the political solution is not so straightforward or simple in spite of the fact that those territories were settled by blacks and, at least theoretically, not open space when whites originally moved in. The whites are also far in the minority in these areas and this seems to support the demand for making black states out of these areas as well.

Has the White Man No Rights?

On the other hand the main body of these white people were genuine settlers, many for generations, and the fact cannot be denied that the development and prosperity of these areas today are wholly the result of their initiative, investment, hard work and administrative capacity. In that sense it is their country, too, or at least parts are, and they or their kin in the mother country have ruled alone until now. Have justice and the demands of morality nothing to say about the primary rights of these white people?

The "Partnership Project"

In the first planning it was accepted that the blacks' rights should be fully protected and the idea of partnership was born. This partnership was, for a long time to come, actually intended to be junior partnership for the blacks and the continued control as senior partner by the whites. Warnings made no impression on the rulers overseas that this theory would not work out that way, with the inevitable result that the black majorities soon demanded, and are quickly receiving, the right to what amounts to full control with the white man pushed out of politics to all intents and purposes.

The white man must, furthermore, expect to lose his possessions and see his hard-won farms, well-developed areas and businesses fall to pieces when he must go, as he realizes is inevitable. It is in such areas that the white settlers feel that they have been left in the lurch by parent countries.

Neither of these solutions would, therefore, suit the already described quite different South African situation. Not only are the whites less outnumbered than anywhere else, and not only do they claim the empty country settled by their forefathers as really theirs, but they know that if they gave way to some preliminary form of partnership it would become the end of white civilization in South Africa, too—and white civilization in the world would lose its only anchor in Africa.

Forget the word "apartheid." Forget any term by which to describe a policy, and just ask yourselves what *you* would do under such circumstances.

Three Possibilities

There are three possibilities. One is that the white nation of South Africa should sacrifice itself, its possessions and the generations to come. They can do this by surrendering to black rule, even if it became a dictatorship, and by evacuating the country of their forebears, or by remaining and becoming an indistinguishable part of a black nation.

Another way is to bluff yourself by making apparently small concessions, hoping to stave off the evil day, so that your children or grandchildren may suffer, but not you. This could be done by accepting some black representatives in Parliament, and in every phase of life in the community, in the hope that their selfish satisfaction of own ambition will prevent them from developing and leading the ambitions of their masses.

And if this does not happen, what then? If junior partnership would quickly — very, very quickly — also lead in South Africa to the demand for black rule alone, must the white man fight or submit? And at what stage should he admit that his subtle attempt to retain power has failed?

In fact, this second method of solving the problem solves nothing at all. It only means that the struggle for power goes on and on, while the white ruler of today lets things develop until he gives in as before, or finds himself at last fighting in the last, or nearly last, ditch for self-preservation.

There is another method, however, and that is to take your example from the nations: live and let live—apart.

We prefer each of our population groups to be controlled and governed by themselves, as nations are. Then they can co-operate as in a commonwealth or in an economic association of nations where necessary. Where is the evil in this? Or in the fact that in the transition stage the guardian must keep the ward in hand and teach him and guide him and check him where necessary? This is our policy of Separate Development.

South Africa will proceed in all honesty and fairness to seek—albeit by necessity through a process of gradualness—peace, prosperity and justice for all by following the model of the nations which in this modern world means political independence coupled with economic interdependence.

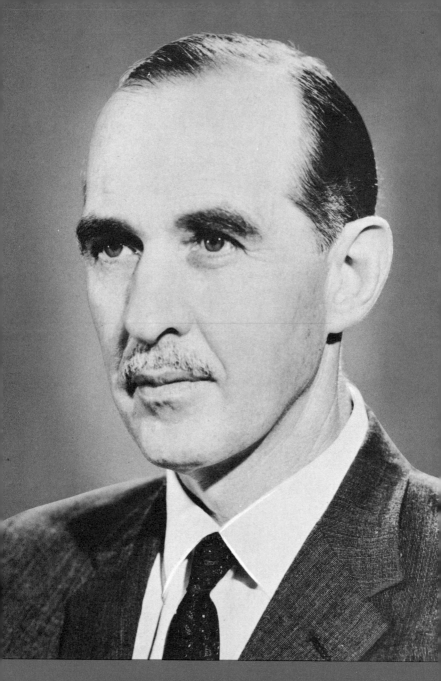

Dr. Hilgard Muller, Foreign Minister of the Republic of South Africa.

Chapter II

Let the World
Take Note

*When he was in New York as a member of the South
African United Nations Delegation, in 1963, Dr. Hilgard Muller, then Ambassador to the United Kingdom,
delivered a speech to the English-Speaking Union in
New York. This talk by Dr. Muller succinctly sets out
the Republic's motivations for embarking on the policy
of Separate Development to meet the challenge posed
by the realities of multi-nationalism in Southern Africa.*

SOUTH Africa today occupies a rather conspicuous position
in international discourse: it is not a singular position
except to the extent that it has been made to appear so. The
position of South Africa in the context of a troubled world
situation is the product of many factors upon which I do not
intend to dwell. All I need say is that the presentation and
interpretation of selected facts about South Africa have led
to the creation of a special image and disproportionate isolation of South Africa's problems.

The result is grotesque: what you see is a cruel caricature
of a country, its people, its Government and a positively
abhorrent image of that country's policy, of the motives
behind it and the mode of its administration.

It should, however, not be very difficult for sober-minded
and responsible people to look objectively at the South African
scene.

South Africa finds itself in the unusual position that many
of her problems are a direct result of growth and expansion;

South Africa has one of the largest oil-from-coal plants in the world. This is a view of the Sasol plant at Sasolburg, Orange Free State.

the country is on the verge of a leap forward towards levels of development and prosperity which far-sighted men failed to foresee even ten years ago.

All this came about as a result of stability, continuity and reliability in government and administration. You could not in any circumstances arrive at a situation of this kind under the impetus of such negative forces as oppression, repression, denial of human rights and the rest of the ills attributed to South Africa.

More than forty years ago a British statesman, Lord Balfour, said that in South Africa a white nation had established itself in the continent of Africa and that this was something that had never before presented itself in the history of mankind.

This fact has been taken for granted for so long that it seems hardly worth mentioning. But recognition of its significance is surely demonstrated by the close links between South Africa and the West and the substantial traffic in trade, investment and immigration, not merely from the United Kingdom and Europe but also from the rest of the free Western world.

It is true that South Africa's withdrawal from the British Commonwealth in 1961 led to the severing of constitutional ties. But many other important ties with the United Kingdom remain strong and cordial. This can also be said of our relations with the other founder-members of the Commonwealth —Canada, Australia and New Zealand. As far as the relationship between South Africa and the United States of America is concerned, they both belong to the Western family of nations and both are integral components of the English-speaking world.

Part of Africa

South Africa is, however, also part of the continent of Africa. On the face of it there may be no mystical significance in the fact that ours is the only state on the continent whose name includes the word "Africa." But for those white people whose home it is, it means that we are of the West in Africa and we are also of Africa in the West.

It is only at this point that I introduce, quite deliberately, the question of relations between the Western or European-descended people in South Africa and the non-Western population groups.

Sea Point, on the Atlantic ocean, is a popular holiday resort in South Africa.

The Wild Coast of the Transkei is famed for its natural rock formations. This is the Hole in the Wall, near Port St. Johns.

This relationship has been arbitrarily placed in a context of crisis and apprehension by people outside South Africa; but since it is, after all, our problem and not theirs, I think that we are better able to judge where this relationship stands in the scheme of things.

I shall endeavour to explain this relationship to you—as we see it. But before doing so I would like to remind you that inter-racial relations present a challenge throughout the world. What many people fail to realize is that such relations, and the problems to which they give rise, vary from one country to another, and that there is therefore no universally applicable solution. The racial set-up in South Africa with which we are dealing has no parallel anywhere in the world — it is *sui generis,* and from this follows that it requires a special solution.

South Africa occupies a curious position in relation to the 19th century "scramble for Africa" by European powers. It was only indirectly linked to this scramble in that its geographical area was included in the scope of the British Imperial design which embraced so much of the rest of Africa.

Resistance to this design resulted in the Anglo-Boer War at the turn of the century. This in turn produced a pattern of constitutional evolution, based on the existence of a white nation in South Africa, which preceded by many years the constitutional and emancipatory developments which took place elsewhere on the continent after the Second World War.

It was thus left to the white nation of South Africa, after its own emancipation from Imperialism, to provide the opportunity, to set the pace and to devise a pattern of emancipation for the non-white population.

The choice was simple enough: There were two alternatives, the first of which was to enter into a constitutional, political, economic and social relationship between the white and non-white population groups that would have placed the white people in a position of effective control, and indeed domination, over all the other national groups—a situation which would not have been incompatible with 19th century practice. The second alternative was to devise a pattern of co-existence which would respond positively to the present-day demands of a world-wide trend towards the elimination of domination of one nation by another and self-determination for even the smaller groupings possessing a national and cultural identity.

The initiative in exercising this choice lay with South Africa's white population, and it was used in favour of the second alternative I have just mentioned.

Real Co-existence

The problem, as I have indicated, was to find a satisfactory pattern for co-existence between the white and non-white population groups in South Africa. The solution suggested to the electorate in the 1948 General Election was Separate Development. It was accepted and it was with that mandate that the present Government of the Republic proceeded to its task.

It is not as if the policy of Separate Development has not been projected by its architects and builders in the idiom of the times. The Prime Minister of South Africa, Dr. H. F. Verwoerd, could hardly have stated the philosophy of his Government's policy in plainer language than the following: *"As long as domination of one race by another exists there will be resistance and unrest. Consequently, the solution should be sought by means of a policy which is calculated to eliminate domination in every form and in every respect."*

Dr. Verwoerd has made many other policy statements in a similar vein, and you will appreciate that these contradict the whole substance of the negative image of South Africa. I therefore do not think that you will find in the files of many newspapers which have for years professed such a tender concern for the well-being of South Africa's population groups, any reference to the statement I have quoted above, or to many others which will clearly invalidate the popular misinterpretation of what the Government in South Africa stands for.

In London in March, 1961, the South African Prime Minister declared: *"We want each of our population groups to control and govern themselves, as is the case with other nations. Then they can co-operate as in a commonwealth—in an economic association with the Republic and each other . . . South Africa will in all honesty and fairness proceed to secure peace, prosperity and justice for all by means of political independence coupled with economic interdependence."*

He elaborated on this projection as follows: "I envisage development along the lines similar to that of the British Commonwealth. In other words, I perceive the development

South Africa has planned its roads with the future in mind. Highways like this one (left) at Cape Town ribbon across the sub-continent.

The Groote Schuur Hospital, Cape Town.

Below: The Baragwanath hospital in South Africa is the largest in the southern hemisphere. Medical services in South Africa for the Bantu are free if they make use of the clinics in the towns.

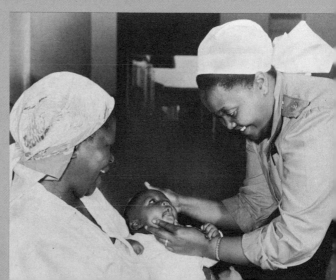

of a Commonwealth of South Africa in which the white State and the black States . . . can co-operate together, without being joined in a federation and therefore without being under a central government but co-operating as separate and independent states. In such an association no state will lord it over any other."

The ideals and ideas enunciated by Dr. Verwoerd point to the destination of his Government's policy. But the translation of such conceptions into practical reality is not the work of a day or a year. We have, as a rule, avoided the stresses and strains of five-year plans and ten-year plans which never seem to come to fruition in any year. Our progress towards the goals outlined by the responsible leader of the Government has been *dictated by the pace at which it is possible to move.*

If we turn now to consider the progress actually achieved, I think you may find it not unimpressive. Many visitors and observers from other countries have been kind enough to say that it has been astonishing.

If our present international position—or if what you have read in your newspapers—has led you to believe my country to be stagnant and sterile, full of desperately unhappy people, filled with hatred for one another—then consider with me the following facts:

Never in her history has the pace of progress been more pronounced or more purposeful than it is at present in South Africa. Never before has the Republic been more prosperous than she is now. The wheels of industry turn faster than they have ever done before—continually oiled by ever larger injections of capital—both domestic and foreign.

Economic Boom

Recently, a report to the United Nations Budget Committee stated that there are only 26 "developed" countries in the world. *In all Africa there is only one such country—and that country is South Africa.* Even now South Africa produces twice as much steel and electricity as the rest of Africa combined. And already work has started on expansion programmes that will double this output within a decade.

The Republic has also embarked upon what will eventually be one of the largest irrigation and hydro-electric projects in the world. The Orange River is to be harnessed in a network of power stations stretching from the Atlantic to the Indian Ocean, bringing water to thousands of farms, to new industries and to towns and cities.

Some 3 billion dollars will be invested in these—and other —projects during the next ten years. All this money can come from our own domestic resources. Most of it will. Some will come from foreign investors. *But not one cent will be foreign aid.*

Meanwhile South Africa continues to produce most of the free world's gold as well as more gem diamonds, more chrome, and more platinum than any other country.

Meanwhile, too, the standard of living of all South Africa's peoples has been rising more rapidly than that of most countries in the world. In fact, in the last decade, *the rate* of increase in the per capita income of all South Africa's citizens equalled that of the United States and Australia, and exceeded those of Canada and New Zealand. A leading economist recently stated that the standard of living in South Africa had doubled in the last forty years, and predicted that the average standard of living for all sections of South Africa's population will be—by the turn of the century—about what it is today for Europe.

It is an undisputed fact that the non-white people of South Africa already have medical services and modern housing which are second to none compared with the rest of the non-white world.

As far as education is concerned, today four out of every five Bantu children are at school. *New schools have been opened at the rate of about one per day.* Already eighty per cent of all Bantu children between seven and twenty years of age, are literate. I am sure you will agree that this is a high rating indeed, in view of the fact that the estimated number of illiterate people in the world today is some 700 million and that the numbers of illiterates elsewhere are still growing by about 20 million a year.

In a highly developed, industrialized country such as South Africa the social progress we are making would, to some degree, have been inevitable, natural and spontaneous.

But only to some degree. Much of what we have achieved has been deliberate policy. For it is *policy* to house and educate South Africa's non-white peoples and to provide them with work. It is *policy* to train them as teachers, doctors, nurses, law enforcement officers, and for the other professions.

This policy has produced one significant fact that is conveniently killed with silence wherever South Africa is internationally arraigned. It is this: those who slip across our borders to escape from our policies are numbered in tens; those who slip across the border to come and enjoy our hospitality are numbered in tens of thousands. We have now no fewer than 800,000 foreign Africans within our borders. We gain about 25,000 every year.

Paradox?

Here, then, we have the perfect paradox of modern international relations. By any criterion South Africa is one of the most successful countries in the world. She is a magnet to tens of thousands of Africans from thousands of miles beyond her borders. She bears no one any malice. She has no hostile intent.

And yet she is subject to formidable pressure from many parts of the world.

Now why should this be?

It is history that provides the answer. For it is history that has afforded South Africa her unique place among the nations of the world. It is history that has carefully — or casually—prepared for her the extraordinary position that she occupies in the world today.

It all began some 300 years ago. At just about the same time as the State of Massachusetts was being established by English settlers, the Dutch established a victualling station at the Cape of Good Hope — half-way between Europe and India and the spice islands.

When the French Huguenots came to South Africa in 1688
they brought with them the art of wine-making which has
become one of South Africa's most important modern industries. The photograph shows a vineyard in the Paarl valley
of the Cape Province.

In both places there were indigenous peoples—in Massachusetts the Indians; in the Cape the Bushmen and Hottentots. The Bushmen still survive. They have taken refuge from civilization and moved to the north where they live their stone-age nomadic lives in peace. Over the years the Hottentots joined with other races and peoples to form the Cape Coloured people of today — a thriving community of some 1,500,000 souls.

One thing above all the two settlements had in common. Both at Massachusetts and at the Cape the settlers introduced a type of social and economic organization that differed absolutely from that of the indigenous peoples. It was *this* organization—developed in Europe—that immediately transformed the very being of these territories and set them—for the first time—on a course of self-perpetuating progress. This was, of course, not exclusive to South Africa or Massachusetts. *It is still one of the facts of history that throughout the "new world" progress has always been in direct proportion to the extent of the European presence: the larger the number of Europeans, the greater was the progress.*

There is another, most remarkable phenomenon—that the two settlements shared. In neither America nor in Africa did the indigenous people adopt the settlers' system, nor the settlers the indigenous system. Individuals did, but the societies remained distinct; the peoples retained their distinctive characteristics and systems.

And it is this phenomenon—above all else—that has been decisive in determining the course of events in South Africa throughout the three centuries that have elapsed since the first settlement at the Cape.

Sporadic Treks

Shortly after the establishment of the victualling station at the Cape the settlers started moving further afield. They crossed one mountain range and then another. They moved from one fertile valley to the next. In their wake they left several tiny settlements. With the years these grew into towns, into cities.

Thus the settlers brought life to the vast South African plains. During all this time they met with no other indigenous people. All was empty. All was no man's land.

It was nearly 150 years later and 600 miles from Cape Town that the white pioneers first came into contact with the vanguard of a black migration which was moving south-

Aerial view of Meadowlands, a huge Bantu township in the Transvaal. Meadowlands was established as part of one of the biggest urban renewal projects in the world. Housing experts from many countries feel that South Africa's progress in this field has been phenomenal. Tenants live in brick houses, pay rentals from between $5 to $8 a month for a family dwelling with all amenities. Conditions attract thousands of "border jumpers" who enter South Africa illegally to share in the welfare services of the country. In the last decade $280 million has been spent on urban renewal—rehousing people in the equivalent of 12 new cities of 100,000 inhabitants each.

wards. These people had set off from somewhere in Central Africa, had come south in wave upon wave of bloodshed, had crossed what are today the northern borders of the Republic and had occupied certain territories on the eastern seaboard of South Africa. They were the Bantu, the ancestors of the black population of South Africa.

When these two migrations met there ensued a long series of wars, mostly in the form of border clashes between them. At the same time the internecine warfare among the various Bantu peoples continued. Such clashes are not peculiar to South African history. One point I might make, though. The wars between black and white were not wars of extermination or conquest. This is why the Xhosa nation of today, for instance, is largely resident in the same areas it had occupied at the end of the 18th century when it first came into contact with European settlement. Similarly in the north of the country there was very little displacement of other Bantu nations. On the contrary, there has taken place in the 20th century what has always been accepted as a temporary "over-spill" of Bantu into areas which had already been settled by Europeans. There is therefore no foundation, whatsoever, for the allegation, so frequently made, that the white man deprived the Bantu in South Africa of land which was traditionally theirs. In fact, for many years the South African Government has augmented the traditional Bantu homelands, which have always been kept intact, by adding to it land which the Government had to purchase from whites.

A century ago there were no more than a million or two Bantu in South Africa. Today there are nearly 12 million. And their numbers are increasing every year.

Of more significance than the wars themselves, however, is this: they were not fought between random collections of individuals, but between *peoples*—peoples with established and vastly disparate systems and organizations; peoples who were all immigrants into what is today South Africa and who over the years had settled different parts of a vast subcontinent.

The hostilities eventually ceased. But there was no blurring of the sharp differences between these distinctive peoples. *The people of European stock refused to compromise with the systems of the Bantu peoples. The Bantu peoples showed no desire to give up their own identity, culture, language and institutions for those of the whites.*

Well tended gardens in Meadowlands Bantu Township near Johannesburg.

South African fruit is canned and exported all over the world.

Not "Colonial Settlers"

By this time the whites had far outgrown their settler status. Those of Dutch and French Huguenot stock had long before cut all ties with the motherland. They were speaking a new language. Above all, there was growing among them a new infant nationalism which later broadened into a South African nationalism and today embraces also the aspirations of the South Africans of British and other European stock.

But let me revert to 1910, the momentous year in which the Union of South Africa — today the Republic of South Africa—was brought into being. The twentieth century was only ten years old and to most of the world's problems solutions were still being dispensed in terms of the nineteenth century doctrine of *laissez faire*. British South Africa was such a problem and the Act of Union such a solution.

In this Union were brought together, on the one hand, the little white nation-to-be and, on the other hand, a host of mutually distinct Bantu peoples. The dispensation came from Europe and the constitution was essentially a European document, primarily intended to compose the differences that remained between Boer and Briton after the Anglo-Boer War.

The Bantu peoples were, of course, also affected by the new constitution, by the new union, but they had no say in it. They were no more than a marginal consideration. That they were distinctive peoples, that some of them, such as the Zulus, even had an established nationhood of their own—that was completely disregarded. They were to be safeguarded, put under tutelage, protected—but they were not to be peoples in their own right.

In all this there was the implied wish—or hope—that in time individual Bantu might be absorbed — into the European society, of course. What was to become of those that remained —that was hardly given a thought.

This political philosophy—this dispensation of affairs—prevailed for several decades after the establishment of Union. The political institutions of South Africa naturally remained geared to the expression only of the European system. The practitioners of this system remained the nation of European stock. Overwhelmingly so. The Bantu people remained on the fringe of things.

It was only in the early post-World War II period that this doctrine of *laissez faire* and its implication of European domination began to be seriously challenged. It was then that Africa was set ablaze in a revolution that sought to cast off all

forms of white overlordship, whether these were beneficial or not. The peoples of Africa demanded to rule their own countries in their own way, to score their own achievements and make their own mistakes. They insisted on self-determination, unfettered and absolute.

They demanded the return of their identity and their dignity—unequivocally, both in deed and in word. They rejected out of hand any philosophy that implied the dismembering of their societies. They ridiculed the prospect of becoming imitation European individuals—the most they could have hoped for until then. They demanded once more to be peoples —African peoples. They discovered, fostered and flaunted the African personality.

Realities

This revolution posed the white nation of South Africa a unique problem of awesome proportions. They could not simply ignore the radical changes in Africa. Their country was, after all, inescapably part of that continent. Sooner or later, therefore, they would have to concede and accept the right to self-determination also of the Bantu peoples or nations within the borders of South Africa.

But history had put them in a position without parallel in Africa. Elsewhere on the continent the response of the colonial powers to the new challenge was a simple one: they withdrew and left the African peoples to rule themselves. But the white South Africans were not "colonialists." *They had by then firmly established their own distinctive nationhood in a homeland that they had not taken from anyone*. They had won their own right to self-determination only a few decades earlier. And this they were not prepared to sacrifice in any circumstances.

For they insisted—and still insist—that self-determination, like liberty, must be indivisible. They argue that if all African nations are entitled to self-determination, then surely their own nation is, too.

Opposite page: top—Grassland contrasts starkly with fenced, protected land, showing the Transkeians the need to protect grazing land.

Middle: Contour plowing on the rolling hills in this high rainfall area prevents soil erosion, a scourge throughout the whole of Africa.

Bottom: A general view of Umtata, capital of the new state.

Timber reaches maturity in the Transkei with its high rainfall
and moderate climate from 5 to 7 times more quickly than in
northern climates. A conservation programme has been carried out for a number of years in an attempt to make the
Transkeians aware of the economic possibilities of timber production. In the past saplings were haphazardly cut down to
make roofing poles for huts, but today the Transkeians operate a timber factory at Vulindlela ("open the doors") which
produces about 700,000 articles annually for local consumption ranging from sophisticated housing material, school desks
to lowly fencing poles.

South Africa was, therefore, faced with this agonizing dilemma: how to provide for the inevitable progress to self-determination of the Bantu nations, without infringing the autonomy of the white nation. How, indeed?

But was there any real choice at all? Indeed, no. For to this problem, posed in this way, history and the realities of Africa dictated only one solution. And that solution was the separate, but full, development of South Africa's peoples. And that, briefly, is what we are attempting to do.

On the one hand the Republic is safeguarding the distinctive nationhood of her people of European stock as history enjoins her to do. At the same time she is helping the various Bantu nations within her borders to find themselves and to be themselves, as the lessons of Africa enjoin her to do.

Transkei

She is aiding these nations to become self-sufficient, ordering their own affairs at all levels of national activity. She sets no ceiling to this development. The aim is viable and autonomous Bantu nations alongside, and in co-operative association with, the white nation. And all these separate nations will have their own historical homelands which had always been exclusively theirs.

So far have we progressed in the implementation of this policy that one of South Africa's Bantu nations in 1962 voted for their own parliament. They are the 3,000,000 Xhosas, whose homeland is the Transkei, in the Eastern Cape.

From the outset the Transkei Government is invested with substantial power to legislate for the territory and its people. And this power will grow, until, sooner or later, the Transkei will be an autonomous state. That is policy.

Meanwhile social and economic progress in the territory is keeping pace with political development. Already five of every six Transkei children are at school and a current program calls for the expenditure by the South African Government of $160 million in the Transkei and other Bantu homelands.

The Xhosas of the Transkei are therefore the first to win their right to self-determination in their historical homeland. They will be followed by other Bantu nations. The die is cast and the political map is being irrevocably redrawn in South Africa.

And it is these developments, too, that the world condemns when it condemns Separate Development.

Above: A cattle show in South Africa. Below: A mixed herd of Bantu livestock near Tsolo. One of the present problems is overgrazing and large tracts are being fenced off and rested.

Some of the critics who condemn our policy maintain that what they want to see in South Africa is a non-racial democracy, which will be neither African nor European in character.

This sounds very *admirable*. But it is not *feasible*. For it flies directly in the face of all the facts of Africa. The reason is simple and obvious. For if Africa has done one thing she has shown conclusively that her peoples have no desire to be recast in a foreign mold.

We must always remember that the way of Africa is not necessarily the way of Europe—or of the West. That is another lesson of Africa. For almost nowhere on that continent have the inherited systems of Europe survived intact for long. Least of all the systems of government.

Far be it from me to say that this is a good thing or a bad thing; that it is right or that it is wrong. After all, no two countries in the world order their affairs in identically the same manner.

As far as the South African nation of European stock is concerned, we are determined to continue to practise the system which is our heritage and has its roots in Western traditions. To ensure this South Africa must be given the opportunity to carry through her policy of Separate Development.

My plea, therefore, is that our friends should make a real endeavour to comprehend the true nature of our problem, the fundamental aims of our policy, i.e. the accommodation, and recognize the tremendous progress we have already achieved. They will then, we firmly believe, take no action which will impede the measures we are taking to bring our policies to fulfillment.

My plea is based on the merits of our policy. For our policy is directly in line with the African revolution, which has as its main objective self-determination for all. In fact, we as the first of the African nationalists anticipated that revolution long before it ever reached the proportions it has today.

At the same time our policy is in accordance with the fundamental philosophies of the West. We do not deny the individuality and dignity of man. What we do say—what our unique situation has taught us to say—is that each man has his dignity and his individuality within the society that he understands, which is his own.

This is our case, our challenge. Therein, too, lies the key to South Africa's relationship with the West, with Africa, and with the world.

South Africa produces about 74 percent of the free world's gold—no mean stabilizer for any economic system. Production is rising annually.

Chapter III

South Africa and the United Nations

The following is an abridged version of a speech presented in the United Nations General Assembly on October 10, 1963, by Mr. G. P. Jooste, Secretary of Foreign Affairs of the Government of South Africa, who was leader of the South African Delegation to the Eighteenth Session. Mr. Jooste is a past Ambassador to the United States and the United Kingdom. He is Special Advisor to the Prime Minister on Foreign Affairs.

THE South African delegation did not come to New York in order to engage other delegations in a dialectic contest. In our view such an approach to international intercourse is sterile. It will get us nowhere, and can only do harm to all concerned. We have often said in the past, and I repeat today, that national pride is not the prerogative of any one nation, or of any single group of nations. To this I would add that truth and justice are not expendable attributes of morality — or fruitful international intercourse.

If we are to have world peace, and if the nations of the world are to live in harmonious circumstances which would enable each one of them to devote its full attention and apply all its resources and energy to the solution of its own peculiar problems, then we shall have to put into practice those concepts which are fundamental in the rules of propriety and justice which must govern the affairs of the international community.

We also have our own views as to what is taking place in the internal lives of other nations. But before coming to any final conclusion, it would be better, and certainly fairer, to ensure that our critics are in possession of all the facts.

Now, what are the main charges against South Africa—charges which have been made despite every effort on our part to demonstrate the false assumptions upon which criticism of our affairs are based? I believe I can summarize them in a single sentence: It is alleged that the South African people of European origin are temporary settlers with no right to a permanent homeland of their own in Africa; that we have taken the country which we claim to be our homeland from

The Parliamentary Assembly of White South Africa in Cape Town.

others and that our Government is therefore an "alien" government: that we seek to maintain our position by coercion and perpetual repression and that our policy, which has been described as one of inherent racial hatred and superiority, is founded on a denial of the right of self-determination: all of which constitute a threat to the peace of the world.

It is true, of course, that *many* of the incorrect statements concerning South Africa's affairs were based, not on hostility, but on real misconceptions—and misinterpretation of the facts. The reason for this may well be that the impact upon the speakers concerned of the often vicious propaganda against us has created an image which others could not but view with disapproval.

Examine Whole Scene

Now, insofar as these delegates are concerned I would only ask them to take a fresh look at the South African scene, and to do so with a greater measure of objectivity—with a more open mind.

The problem which overshadows the South African scene and which must be given the highest priority in our domestic policies, is the relationship between the South African nation of European descent and the many Bantu nations who presently live under the sovereignty of the South African Government. This is the problem of which we must *first of all* dispose before we can give our entire attention to such residual problems which affect other, smaller population groups. This does not mean that these problems, which I have termed "residual problems," do not receive attention. They do. Indeed they receive our constant attention; but we will be able to deal with them much more effectively after we have dealt with the position of the great numbers of Bantu who constitute several distinct and separate nations.

Africa not only home of Black men

In order to achieve a proper understanding of the position it is necessary to recognize the fundamental fact that Africa is not the exclusive preserve of any one race—whatever the general image may be. Africa has over the millennia of history been the home of many widely differing nations. There is no single African race—just as little as there is a single Asian race, or a single American race. This is a fact of history which must always be borne in mind.

The European population established itself on the Southern tip of Africa more than three centuries ago—without in any way possessing land occupied by others. As for the Bantu

people, they were migrating southward down the coast of Eastern South Africa; and it was nearly 150 years after the first white settlement that these two main groups met.

When this happened border clashes took place periodically during the first half of the 19th century, yet, despite this the Xhosa nation of today is largely resident in the same areas as it occupied at the end of the 18th century when it first came into contact with white settlement. Similarly in the North of what is today South Africa there was very little displacement of other Bantu nations. On the contrary, there has taken place in the present century what has always been accepted as a temporary "over-spill" of Bantu into areas which had already been settled by white Africans. There is therefore no foundation for the allegation, so frequently made, that the white African deprived the Bantu in South Africa of land which was traditionally theirs. In fact, for many years the white South African Government has augmented the traditional Bantu homelands, which have been kept intact, by adding land which the Government purchased from white Africans.

It is against this background and in this perspective that our situation, and what is being done with regard to it, must be viewed.

White Africans

The fact which emerges (fundamental to our position on the African continent) is that the South Africans of European origin have been forged into a single and distinctive nation. It is no longer a European nation, although it is closely linked with Western culture and civilization. *It is a nation of Africa, with roots and traditions deeply embedded in the soil of that continent. These roots cannot be destroyed and the white South Africans claim for themselves all the inalienable rights of an autonomous and separate nation.* They further claim the right to live and to manifest themselves as a nation with its own distinctive identity—a fundamental right which, as must all other nations who wish to survive, they will defend by every means at their disposal.

It is true, of course, that today this nation of Western stock has an over-all responsibility for promoting the welfare and progress of all those who live under the sovereignty of its Government. This has been the process of history. But, it is

Chief Minister Matanzima has announced that waterfalls will be harnessed to supply hydro electric power for the whole area together with the future possibility of coal mining to produce electric power. The Transkei offers great opportunities for sustaining industrial expansion.

Bantu university graduates at the conclusion of a graduation ceremony.

The Xhosa also have another graduation ceremony—that of the Abakwetha when young men are initiated into tribal life and responsibility.

essential that in claiming for ourselves a distinctive destiny of our own, *we do not* deny to the emerging Bantu nations their right to achieve distinctive destinies of their own—each in his own homeland with its own culture, heritage, language and concept of nationhood. This is fundamental in our approach to the problem; and the Bantu are beginning, more and more, to accept the fact that the South African Government will always endeavour to promote these rights as moral and inalienable rights.

Nations Are Not Interchangeable

In South Africa, natural differences—i.e., the different attributes and identities (and not the superiority or the inferiority of any one of these nations) which exist between the various national communities, have proved to us, over the centuries, that there can be no real and permanent accommodation in the circumstances which obtained in the past. A permanent accommodation can, therefore, only be found if each of the South African nations is afforded the opportunity of achieving full nationhood with full political responsibility within its own homeland.

In this connection we of Western origin are fortified in the pursuit of our aims by the lesson of history that the domination of one nation over another cannot afford a *permanent* solution.

Many statements by our Prime Minister outline the fundamentals of South African policy. In 1960 he stated:

> *"The essential condition (to a stable and prosperous country) is that racial domination will have to be removed. As long as domination of one race by another exists there will be resistance and unrest. Consequently the solution should be sought by means of a policy which is calculated to eliminate domination in every form and in every respect."*

> *In March, 1961, Dr. Verwoerd said:*
> *"We do not only seek and fight for a solution which will mean our survival as a white race, but we also seek a solution which will ensure survival and full development —politically and economically—to each of the other racial groups as well, and we are prepared to pay a high price out of our earnings to ensure their future.*

> *"The moral problem, just like the political problem, is to find a way out of the extremely difficult and complicated situation caused by the fact that no longer is the black man incapable or undesirous of participation in the control of his destiny. Nor is there any longer anyone pre-*

pared to refuse the fulfillment of such ambitions in a form that is fair to all."

The Prime Minister went on to say:

"We want each of our population groups to control and to govern itself as is the case with other nations. Then all can co-operate as in a Commonwealth — in an economic association with the Republic and with each other . . . South Africa will proceed in all honesty and fairness to secure peace, prosperity and justice for all by means of political independence coupled with economic inter-dependence."

In another statement the Prime Minister said:

"I envisage development along lines similar to that of the (British) Commonwealth. In other words, I perceive the development of a Commonwealth of South Africa in which the White State and the Black States can co-operate together, without being joined in a federation, and therefore without being under a central government, but co-operating as separate and independent States. In such an association no State will lord it over any other. They will live rather as good neighbours."

The South African Government's objective is to achieve the political independence of the various Bantu nations within their homelands—and thus also to eliminate domination in every form and in every respect, as well as to enable the present Bantu homelands to develop into separate Bantu Nation States.

I have quoted our Prime Minister's words on the aim of achieving an association based on the commonwealth pattern of co-operating states. This would forge a link which would establish permanent contact, as good neighbours, and co-operation with regard to the many matters of common concern. As Dr. Verwoerd said:

". . . seeing that we want to develop those areas for them (i.e. the Bantu), can you not understand that we shall bring discrimination to an end by coming together and consulting at a high level on the basis of equality, of equal human dignity through the establishment, for example, of a Commonwealth Conference of our own?"

Mr. President, here we now have the Government's policy insofar as the charge of "perpetual domination" is concerned, and the manner in which we are striving towards a future which holds out hope of survival, of complete political independence, and of realistic contacts and co-operation. Here we also have the essence of orderly and planned self-determination.

We have often been accused that however realistic and moral our policy may sound when it is described in terms which I have employed, the question remains as to whether we are in earnest to achieve the proclaimed objectives. We have long since realized that, having regard to the image which has been created outside the confines of our own country—we will, in the final analysis, have to rely on practical achievements—that we will have to produce concrete results in order to convince the world of our *bona fides* as well as of the realism and practicability of what we have set out to achieve.

Prototype

This evolution of self-government in the Transkei provides a prototype for the development of self-government in other Bantu homelands, but since the patterns in South Africa are so diverse the arrangements may not be identical and will have to be adapted by the Bantu to the needs and the aspirations of their emerging nations. For every Bantu nation the issue of ultimate self-determination is a fully accepted objective of Government policy.

Here is real proof of what we are trying to do—and I leave it to all delegates of good will to judge whether our policy is doomed to failure—or whether the Government of my country should not be given an opportunity to proceed along these lines which, as must be evident, could well be the accommodation of a unique problem requiring a unique approach.

Racism?

I would like to add that the suggestion that South African policy derives from, or is inspired by, racial hatred, does not bear even a superficial examination. The allegation emanates largely from those who are influenced by passions which are familiar to them in their own environment but who know nothing about the South African scene. It derives also from the campaign conducted against us — in many cases by subversive forces — whose activities inside South Africa we are obliged to combat by appropriate means — as is done in all countries.

No serious critic with a full knowledge of the South African situation, however honest his criticisms may be in other respects—can legitimately subscribe to the thesis that the concept of Separate Development is founded on hatred of the Bantu. On the contrary, every South African concerned with policy-making understands only too well that friendship and mutual respect provide the only sound basis on which to build a healthy relationship between the White and Bantu nations.

Above: A vast land reclamation project has been launched in the Transkei. More than 14,000 miles of fencing have been put up to protect the lands against heavy grazing. Bales of barbed wire outside Umtata before dispatch to the country areas. Lower picture: Crop rotation and the introduction of western type products are some of the features of this agricultural project—a Bantu farmer tends his cabbages.

We Will Succeed

Equally wrong is the charge that the white South African nation is endeavouring to entrench its position because of fear. Let me assure this Assembly that fear is not an element in the motivation of our policies. Our Government is confident that it will ultimately succeed in its task. Had it not been for this absolute confidence, based as it is on our knowledge of our own affairs, we could not have withstood, for so long, the incredible onslaught on us both in and outside this Organization.

It is not conflict we desire but peace—peace in order to proceed with our great task—a task which requires all our resources, energy, and time.

Moreover, we want to live in peace and co-operate with all other countries—including those who are in Africa. In our relations with these African countries co-operation in all matters of common concern was always a fundamental aim in South African policy. That this is so we have already demonstrated in a tangible way. They, however, have seen fit now to deny us the opportunity of continuing the co-operation which proved so fruitful in the past.

This co-operation has covered a wide range of technical problems and assistance has been rendered on a considerable scale—for example by the world famous Veterinary Laboratory at Onderstepoort, the South African Institute for Medical Research, the Bureau of Standards, the Council for Scientific and Industrial Research and many other technical institutes. Millions of vaccines have been despatched to various African countries and there has been a regular exchange of visits between technical experts. In 1960-62 South African experts made 40 visits to 11 African States and in the same period experts from 15 African States paid more than 60 visits to South Africa. Even now South Africa contributes by way of financial aid and expert advice to combat agricultural problems in other African States.

Maturity Takes Time

Although much of this technical collaboration has recently been rejected by the other African States it is possible that as time passes, and as they achieve a clearer perception of our true aims, in our own country and in our contacts beyond our frontiers, wiser counsel will prevail and that co-operation in all fields of common concern will be resumed. For, we are confident that, given the proper opportunity and atmosphere, we shall be able to make a material contribution in the pursuit of the orderly and peaceful development of Africa.

THE PATTERN OF PARTITION

Mr. M. C. Botha, Minister of Bantu Administration and Development, speaking at the 1966 meeting of the South African Bureau of Racial Affairs stated that there was still much to be done in the way of consolidating the various Bantu areas before the ultimate aim of their geographic partition was reached.

The Minister spoke on the theme 'the future of the whites in South Africa,' and said the survival of the white man in South Africa depended to a great extent on the white man giving to the Bantu that which he demanded for himself, namely an own national autonomy.

Because the white man was presently in a more privileged position and better developed than the Bantu, it was the duty not only to place the Bantu on the road to becoming a national entity, but also to help the Bantu to promote this. The whites could therefore strengthen their own position by assisting the Bantu in their development.

"It is essential in the interests of all, that we should renew our dedication to the visions of separate development for each of the various peoples which we believe have been placed

here by providence. Let us not shirk the consequences of separation or differentiation.

"As far as White-Bantu relations were concerned, there was already total separation in the political sphere but consideration should be given to the immensity of the task of giving geographic entity to the various separated Bantu homelands.

"Much had yet to be done in consolidating the various areas and in obtaining land earmarked for the Bantu. There were some enthusiasts who urged immediate partition.

"Our work is after all aimed at ultimate geographic partition. Therefore, I much prefer willingness on the part of everyone on every day that dawns, to let justice be done in the consolidation of the homelands and that which is consistent, essential and above all, unavoidable."

The whites of South Africa should never take their survival for granted, the Minister said. "In these times of material prosperity, it is very necessary to be on guard against spiritual and intellectual decline as a result of comfort and a desire for luxury. What lies ahead for us is hard work and sweat and self-assertion on a steep and difficult road—not the easy open road which many imagine as a road of slack passiveness. Our choice is therefore—a struggle for life or the peace of death.

"The future of the whites in South Africa had become inseparable from relations with others, including the many territories on the African continent which had become independent in the past decade.

"The existence and survival of a people is constantly tied up with the existence of other peoples and no people can disregard this. What however, is important to the whites and their future, is that there should be continual adjustments to changing circumstances."

The greatest challenge of all time to the whites in the Republic is in the present circumstances to make adjustment without sacrificing their own identity, the Minister said.

"By way of summary I wish to emphasize that the survival of the whites as a people does not lie in isolation but in the pattern of multi-national coexistence. Successful coexistence depends on good neighborliness which must be promoted at all times and all levels.

"The whites are prepared to make concessions and adjustments but they are not prepared to sacrifice their national identity and by the same token they do not expect any other people in Africa to do this."

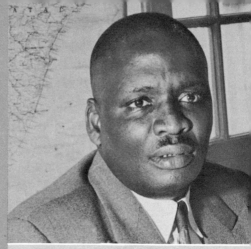

Mr. E. M. Mbuli—Treasurer of the former Transkeian Territorial Authority. Mr. Mbuli, a qualified lawyer, is typical of the men employed in administrative positions by the Transkeian Government.

Mr. S. Dazama, a Bantu sub-inspector of schools in the Transkei. Mr. Dazama has been teaching for forty years and has a number of educational publications to his credit.

Mr. P. Makongwana, another of the Bantu sub-inspectors of the Transkeian educational system.

Chapter IV

Transkei Prototype

In the following chapter is an abridged version of the argument delivered in the South African Parliament by Mr. M. D. C. de Wet Nel, a former Minister of Bantu Administration and Development when he introduced the second reading debate on the Bill to grant self-government to the Transkei.

THIS Bill is the logical projection of the pattern and policy of the people of South Africa with regard to our multinational situation—a policy not created out of political hallucinations or ideologies, but which has grown systematically out of experience and knowledge over a period of more than three centuries of contact with African realities.

It is founded on a simple but basic formula for personal happiness and human relations, namely, that every person is at his happiest within his own family circle; that every family is at its happiest within its own community, and every community is at its happiest within its own national environment. This principle holds true for all people irrespective of race or colour throughout the whole world. It is even more applicable to the Bantu (blacks) because, as any anthropologist can testify, this is one of the basic characteristics in the social structure of the Bantu.

Paternalism or Common Sense?

Furthermore, it should be remembered that our nation's approach to its multi-national situation is not the result of the whims of so-called world opinion, or of opportunistic considerations of self-interest, but the fruit of our attitude to life—with its predominant approach of "live and let live."

- Our people never enslaved the Bantu
- Our nation saved the Bantu from large-scale internecine extermination and created order out of primitive chaos

- We recognized the homelands of the Bantu national groups, protected them against white penetration and later extended them

- We protected the riches of the Bantu territories against white exploitation; guarded against over-cropping and preserved them for the Bantu

- To the best of our ability we helped the Bantu to develop spiritually and materially:

  (a) The best of Western civilization was placed at their disposal

  (b) Relatively speaking, no nation anywhere in the world has done as much for the welfare and happiness of its non-white population as the South Africans

  (c) Our churches spend a great amount on mission work among the Bantu

- We did not follow a policy of denationalization of the Bantu. Our policy is expressly aimed at preventing alienation from one's own community, and at encouraging the principle of service to and building of one's own national community.

- We believe, however, that these groups should benefit from the fruits of what is best in Western civilization.

- We refuse to bundle them together to satisfy our own selfishness, and will not allow disintegration to be brought about for reasons of our own self-interest.

- We have always believed that they should be aided systematically towards managing their own affairs, while they determine their own paths.

Stability and Progress

When we regard the chaotic conditions now reigning in other parts of Africa, we are even more convinced that we are on the right road. The fact remains that whereas elsewhere in Africa disorder and chaos reign, South Africa experiences tranquility and peace. Whereas economic retrogression exists there, *we* have the greatest measure of stability and economic progress. It is still possible in South Africa for white and black to confer peacefully over our mutual future.

This Bill offers the clearest possible proof that we are in earnest about Separate Development and that when we say we grant the Bantu that which we demand for ourselves it is not mere lip-service. We are really prepared to implement our policy fully and create for the Bantu the opportunity to manage his own affairs in accordance with his own abilities in the political sphere, within his own homeland, and so to work out his own future. Moreover, white South Africa, as befits a friend, is prepared to assist the Bantu to the best of its ability in all spheres, also administratively and financially, in order to make a success of this political development in Bantu territory — an evolvement only made possible now after sound preliminary work and the laying of a solid foundation upon which the future can be built.

The main objection is that with our policy we are carving up the country. I wish to state that this is by no means the case, but that this Bill is strictly in accordance with the traditional policy of the country as formulated and applied for generations. The Bill actually gives expression to two great principles in our traditional Bantu policy towards which nearly all statesmen of note had worked to a greater or lesser degree:

Firstly, that the Bantu should have his own homeland which should be reserved and protected; and

Secondly, that the Bantu should in these homelands receive a growing measure of self-government. There have been differences about the manner, degree and time of self-government, e.g. whether it should be according to the Western pattern or an extension of the traditional Bantu system of administration.

Historical Background—Real, not Artificial Partition

In support of my statement that these two cornerstones of our policy have for generations been generally accepted, advocated and applied in South Africa, not only by Republican governments but also by various British governments, I wish, to stress the following:

(i) That the Bantu areas of the Ciskei between the Great Fish River and the Great Kei River were demarcated by the British Government as far back as 1878;

(ii) That the present-day Transkei, from the earliest times, has been regarded as a purely Bantu area and that it

has retained its identity as a Bantu area since its annexation by the Cape Colony in 1879;

(iii) That as far back as 1839 the Voortrekkers started with the demarcation of areas in Natal, and this was continued by the British Government from 1843:

(iv) That separate areas were demarcated and allocated to the Natal Native Trust in 1864, while in 1897 Zululand was incorporated into Natal though retaining its identity;

(v) That in the Transvaal a start was made with demarcation of land to tribes in 1853 and that a standing Natives Location Commission in 1861 commenced defining these areas;

(vi) That the Orange Free State also recognised the principle of separate Bantu areas and in 1867 allocated Witsieshoek to the Mopeli and Batlokoa tribes, while Thaba 'Nchu was reserved in 1884 for the Barolong.

Apart from smaller splinter areas, the following main areas occupied by the different Bantu national groups, existed at the end of the 19th century: Vendaland in the far Northern Transvaal occupied by the Venda; parts of the Letaba area by the Tsonga; Sekhukhuneland in the Northern and North-Eastern Transvaal by the North Sotho; Bechuanaland with the inclusion of parts of the North-West Cape and Western Transvaal by the Tswana; Basutoland with the inclusion of Witsieshoek and parts of the Northern Transkei by the South Sotho; Swaziland with the inclusion of parts of Barberton, Piet Retief and Northern Zululand by the Swazi; Zululand and certain other parts of Natal by the Zulu, and the Transkei together with parts of the Ciskei by the Xhosa. Of these, the following Bantu areas were already clearly demarcated; Xhosaland, Zululand, Swaziland, Basutoland and Bechuanaland. The latter three were at that stage already recognized as separate Bantu territories.

At the founding of Union in 1910 the British Government kept three large Bantu areas Bechuanaland*, Basutoland† and Swaziland with a total area one-third the size of British South Africa, outside the Union, and thus indicated that these areas should be maintained as Bantu areas. After the coming into being of Union, the Union Government immediately, by means of legislation, entrenched as such the areas already acknowledged by its predecessor as Bantu areas, by

---

* Now independent state of Botswana
† Now independent state of Lesotho

This bridge was built entirely by Transkeians to serve their state's ever-growing transport requirements.

Interior of a Bantu home at the Daveyton Bantu township on the East Witwatersrand.
Medical services for the Bantu in South Africa are free if they make use of the clinics. South Africa's medical services are far in advance of those of other African countries. The ratio of doctors to population is highest on the continent.

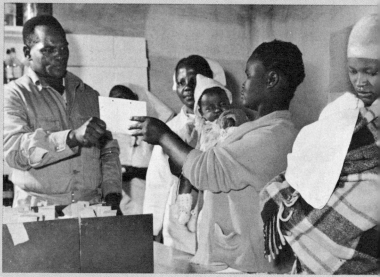

incorporating these in terms of the Natives Land Act of 1913. But the Union government did not leave it at that. A further 15,840,000 acres of land were made available for systematic addition to the Bantu areas and of this nearly 10,555,600 acres have already been added, not as "re-payment" for white settled land but in pursuance of the desire to see the Bantu homelands become even more viable.

The four areas comprising the present-day Transkei, namely the actual historic Transkei, i.e. Fingo- and Gcalekaland; Tembuland, and Pondoland, were as a result of either armed conflict or voluntary agreement, placed under British rule between the years 1877 and 1894. We must, however, make the point very clear that the majority of these areas in the Transkei were placed under British rule not as a result of armed conflict but as a result of mutual agreement. The Bantu tribes under leadership of the Chieftains of that time requested the British government to take their areas under its protection to *preserve their lands for themselves and their descendants.*

As a result these areas were never utilised for any large scale white settlement, but were regarded as entirely Bantu land which should be protected for the Bantu and preserved for them. When the South African Native Trust was created in 1936 and took over Bantu land in trust, it was clearly stated in this act that the Trust should be administered for the *settlement, maintenance, and material as well as moral welfare of the Bantu of the Union.* We have always realized that we managed this land only as trustees or guardians, but that the land *belongs to the Bantu.* South Africa has a clean record and clear conscience in these matters; we did not misuse our position of trust, but over a period of generations we have preserved the Bantu's territory for him and managed it to the best of our ability for his benefit, enlightenment and progress. Are we now doing wrong by saying "yes" to the Bantu when he says that he has arrived at the stage where he would like to manage this land himself? I am rather of the opinion that if we should refuse we could then be accused of dishonesty and unlawful appropriation. We want to, and will, give to the Bantu that which is his and which rightfully belongs to him.

Have I not the right to ask then: Why are we now being accused of "cutting up and dividing" the country? Has our country not already been divided by history? Were these lands not set aside by history? And has it not since been recognized and respected by all responsible people in the country as Bantu Territory?

Self-Government

I now come to the second great principle which has always been generally accepted by our people and its recognized leaders, and that is that the Bantu must obtain self-government in his own homelands. No one with any knowledge of history will oppose this thesis. To be sure, development and application of this principle was sporadic and often full of inconsistencies, but the fact remains that everyone shared this view and tried to put it into practice. Let me briefly draw your attention to the following historical developments of the past:

  (i) It was for many years the general policy of the early Cape Colony and the Voortrekkers (pioneers) in Natal, the Orange Free State and the Transvaal to conclude treaties with chiefs.

 (ii) The well-known administrative policy of Sir Theophilus Shepstone in Natal from 1846 was chiefly based on the extension and development of the existing tribal system.

(iii) Then there was the well-known system of local government with its local and location councils which was instituted under the Glen Grey Act of 1894 and was gradually extended to the Transkei—eventually to result in the formation of the "United Transkeian Territories General Council" in 1930.

(iv) Since the time of Union a series of Acts have been passed which recognize this principle, of which the Bantu Authorities Act of 1951 is perhaps the most important. It was followed by the Promotion of Bantu Self-Government Act of 1959.

The policy of granting self-government to the Bantu in his homelands in South Africa is nothing new. Indeed, it is just as much an accepted part of our traditional Bantu policy as is the reservation of separate homelands for the Bantu.

I will go further, however, by drawing attention to the fact that all our recognized leaders since 1910 have pleaded this idea of separate Bantu homelands and self-government for the Bantu in those homelands. In order to illustrate the accordance of views on the matter I need only quote the various Prime Ministers of this country since 1910.

1. During the second reading debate on the Native Trust Bill of 1913, the then Prime Minister, General Louis Botha, made the following significant statement: "The people must be helped in their development and the preservation

of their traditions. They have their own traditions as do the whites and we must not try to make whites of them. We must take their position and traditions into account and not mix them together. If the Native is separated he must be given the right to govern himself."

2. General Smuts, too, in a speech at the Savoy Hotel in London on 22 May, 1917, expressed the following significant views. "It may be that on those parallel lines we may yet be able to solve a problem which may otherwise be insoluble." And further on: "Thus in South Africa you will have in the long run large areas cultivated by blacks and governed by blacks, where they will look after themselves in all their forms of living and development, while in the rest of the country you will have your white communities, which will govern themselves separately according to accepted European principles."

3. In a speech made by General Hertzog on December 3, 1925, in Pretoria, he was reported as follows by "Die Burger" of the following day—"The Native should be able to feel at home within the Native areas. He should, therefore, not be subject to any restrictions other than those which are necessary in every approved group of people. It is my intention that in so far as he is able, and in accordance with civilized practices, he should be able to lay down his own rules whereto he must conform in his area ... *but I do not only wish him to be his own legislator within his own national household; he must also conduct his own administration by means of his own native powers*. There will thus be an opportunity in the native area for native statesmen as well as for native officials."

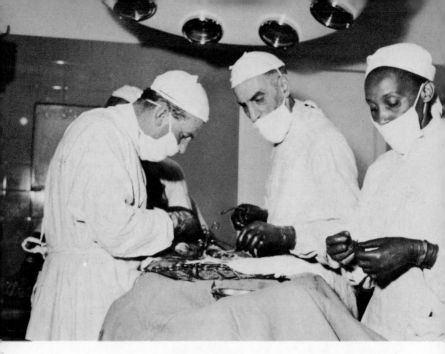

Medical services in South Africa are superior to those elsewhere on the African continent. Above: An operation being performed in a Bantu Hospital. Below: The Efata school for blind Bantu children near Umtata.

4. In 1948 the policy of the National Party under the leadership of Dr. Malan was published. It stated, inter alia:

   "In their own areas the non-white racial groups will receive full opportunities for development in all walks of life. The Native reserves must become the true homeland of the Natives."

5. On 25 August, 1955 Mr. Strijdom addressed the congress of the Natal National Party at Vryheid and expressed his policy as follows—"The purpose of the apartheid policy is that, by separating the races in every field in so far as it is practically possible, one can prevent clashes and friction between whites and non-whites. At the same time, in fairness to the non-whites, they must be given the opportunity of developing in their own areas and in accordance with their own nature and abilities under the guardianship of the whites; and, in so far as they develop in accordance with the systems which are best adapted to their nature and traditions, to govern themselves there and serve their community at all the various levels of their national life."

This Bill, to grant self-government to the Bantu of the Transkei, is nothing new. In fact it is founded on two of the most generally acknowledged and accepted cornerstones of our Bantu policy in South Africa: to recognize separate areas for the Bantu and to grant them powers of government there.

Since then the National Government has conscientiously and systematically carried out this mandate. Since 1948 the new Government continued to implement its policy step by step and a course had been taken which left no illusions with Whites or non-Whites about the Government's policy and objects. *Separate Development is a great idea and we have no doubt that to carry it out will require time and all our strength but we were absolutely determined, and I think we can justly say today, and friend and foe will admit it, that this Government was not deterred from its course by pressure from within or from without our country. We have continued consistently on our course—the traditional road of our nation.*

Another extremely important point I wish to state emphatically is that the responsible Bantu in South Africa, that is to say, the great mass, are increasingly fixing their hopes on the policy of Separate Development in spite of all the frightening tales and incitement, because it brings about prosperity and peace for them, too, and creates the opportunity for development in all spheres of life, free from unfair common contest.

The policy of parallel development in the Transkei resulted in the replacement of white officials by Transkeians. A Transkeian postmaster in his office at Umtata.

Patients in the Tembuland tuberculosis hospital making curios, which are sold to tourists.

Consultation—Details

In regard to the granting of self-government to the Transkei, the wheel was set in motion by the Bantu of that homeland themselves. They, of all the Bantu territories, have perhaps had the longest experience of participation in the control of their own affairs. They realized the advantages and possibilities which the policy of parallel development holds in store for them too. Therefore, I must also point out another very important aspect of this Bill of which sight should not be lost when this matter is discussed, and that is, that this Bill is pre-eminently the fruit of consultation with the Bantu of the Transkei themselves.

Often in the past—and even today—the Government of the Republic has been accused in certain circles of a lack of "consultation" with the Bantu. We repeatedly rejected this accusation in the past and proved it to be false, and we were always able to show that constant and intimate consultation exists with the Bantu on matters of interest to him and that we even established special machinery for consultation.

However, it may perhaps serve a good purpose when we now say specifically for the consumption of those who always glibly accuse us of a lack of consultation, how this Bill came into being. As is generally known, the Transkeian Territorial Authority during its ordinary session in May, 1961, appointed a Recess Committee of 27 members, consisting of 14 chiefs and 13 ordinary councillors to consider the possibilities and implications of self-government for the Transkei. After the Committee had been engaged in its task for a number of months, the executive committee of the Territorial Authority met Dr. H. F. Verwoerd and myself in Pretoria in December of that year. On that occasion, certain problems were discussed and the Prime Minister stated clearly that the Government was prepared to consider favourably the Territorial Authority's request for self-government, and the assistance of officials was offered if the Committee should find such assistance necessary for the successful execution of its task. At the following meeting of the Recess Committee at Umtata on January 31 a number of officials attended and certain principles regarding self-government were formulated. Afterwards a preliminary report was compiled and this report and its implications were again discussed with the Prime Minister and myself at Pretoria on March 19. Thereafter, the Recess Committee met at Umtata on March 30, 1962, and its report was completed. Thereupon, some sixty representatives of the Transkeian Bantu in the big urban centers were invited to Umtata during April, 1962, to discuss the recommendations of the Committee, and to obtain their views on the matter. The

Above: Hill behind Science Building at Turfloop University contains collection of Northern Transvaal flora.

Below: The Bantu are producing scientists to aid in the development of their nations.

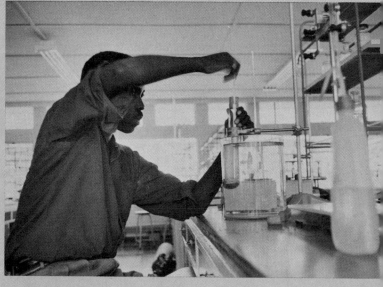

report was distributed in the Transkei itself and discussed with the local inhabitants. At the end of April the report was discussed by the full Territorial Authority and virtually unanimously accepted. The Territorial Authority requested the Government to draft a Bill for the provision of self-government in the Transkei based on the recommendations contained in the report and to the extent to which the report was acceptable to the Government. This was done and, as you know, this Bill was taken back to the Transkei and from December 11 it was discussed in detail at a special session of the Territorial Authority.

If ever there was a matter of interest for the Bantu in this country in regard to which they co-operated more actively and were consulted and recognized to a greater extent, even on the highest level of government, then I should like to hear about it. I want to go further and say that I doubt whether the political development in any other emancipated state in Africa has taken place with such a degree of open-hearted consultation, with such a degree of mutual trust, and such a measure of unanimity as in this instance.

Bantu's Own Creation

Now I wish to emphasize another important fact that this Bill was the creation of the Bantu in the Transkei. We assisted them where necessary. However, it was they who put it into shape. It will be to their credit, because throughout they showed a spirit of application, responsibility and dignity. How different this was compared with constitution-making in other parts of Africa! Here the matter was dealt with in a spirit of cordiality and co-operation in the minimum of time to the great satisfaction of the Transkein people, while elsewhere it took months of strife and bitterness which only resulted in new problems, and most of the countries concerned are steering towards dictatorship.

This Bill is not a slavish copy of constitutions of Western democracy, but it bears its own Bantu imprint—a Bantu imprint that in no way derogates from the best principles of democracy, but which rather makes an active contribution to making democratic government strike firm roots.

The Constitution

A unicameral system is recommended for the Transkei. Various alternatives were considered in this connection, among which the proposal that there should be two houses, viz. a legislative assembly (Congress) and an Upper House

(Senate) and that the chiefs should take their seats in the Upper House. However, these proposals were unanimously defeated, and among the most important reasons mentioned were the following:

(a) According to Bantu tradition it is correct that the chief and his subjects should gather to decide on the affairs of the nation;

(b) In Bantu law the chief-in-council is the legislator of the people and he should, therefore, have a share in the legislative assembly itself;

(c) The chiefs are the traditional governors of the people. Among the Bantu they definitely have the most experience in managerial matters and the exercising of power. As in the past, it is imperative that they should actively participate in administrative matters.

(d) Experience elsewhere has taught that where the chiefs are pushed aside it leads to the downfall and elimination of the traditional authority; and instead of this resulting in the creation of a Western democratic system, as intended, a Western mantle is hung about a system which in reality, is superseded by autocratic dictatorship.

Composition of Legislative Assembly

There were a great variety of proposals in regard to this matter, and many different formulas were actually considered. It has already been stressed there were no objections against members of the Legislative Assembly being elected by the Bantu, and when initially a large proportion of traditional members—as against elected members—was in fact proposed the Prime Minister himself indicated that in his opinion *the ratio was too much in favour of the traditional members*. The matter was then reconsidered by the Recess Committee and the present formula was decided on which works out at more or less 60 per cent traditional members as against 40 per cent elected members. The fact that there will now be elected members in the Legislative Assembly is also no deviation from the policy of developing the traditional administrative system because the Bantu's development will be organic and not artificial.

As far as the ratio and the composition of the Legislative Assembly itself is concerned, the following considerations were taken into account:

(a) For the reason already mentioned it was decided that chiefs and elected members should assemble in one House.

(b) Because of the fact that the chiefs are the traditional legislators and rulers of the Bantu and have had the most experience in managerial affairs and the maintenance of authority, they should have a majority in the house, otherwise things might lead to a total degeneration of the traditional system known to the Bantu.

(c) Taking these facts into account it was decided that a ratio of 60 against 40 at this stage gives sufficient protection to the traditional system and still offers sufficient opportunity for the participation in, and advancement of, the managerial body by elected members. This was done after the South African Prime Minister had suggested that there should be a greater percentage of elected representatives.

(d) Since all the existing chiefs represent separate tribal units or ethnic groups, it was decided not to interfere with the traditional right of these groups to be represented in the legislative assembly by their traditional tribal chiefs. Therefore, it was decided that all the 64 existing chiefs must be members of the legislative assembly and that the remaining 45 members should be elected.

(e) These elected members are by the Transkeian citizens in the Transkei, as well as by those Transkeians in the rest of the Republic, and arrangements will be made which will offer full opportunities to register and to vote to all Transkeian citizens throughout the Republic.

The Position of the Chief

The Bill contains various stipulations concerning chieftainship. These are patterned on the tribal system. *For example, chiefs and all tribal authorities will retain their existing duties, powers and functions until such time as their own legislative assembly brings about changes therein—everything, of course, is designed to break as little as possible with the past and what is known to the Bantu.* Paramount chiefs' personal status in their own areas will be protected, whilst the existing ethnical classification in nine main groups will be maintained—even during the election of members—and each tribal region will form a separate constituency.

The indication throughout is that we and the Bantu are building here on the good of the past, and that Bantu tradition is being taken into account and protected all the way through.

Election of Ministers

Provision is made for the election of the Chief Minister (Prime Minister) as well as the Ministers *by the Legislative Assembly.* This is a new concept in formation of the executive branch of a government but was done at the request of the recess committee. The most important considerations for this step were:

    (a) The fact that it is in accordance with the Bantu managerial system;

    (b) because it will ensure a greater general trust in the Chief Minister.

Every nation gives form and shape to its own political and philosophical ideas of state. I have no doubt that this system is a valuable contribution to the development of politics in Africa and the world. Let us remember that no form of Government prefabricated and *forced upon a nation from outside has any hope of succeeding.*

Separate Citizenship

A further outstanding feature of this Bill is to create a distinctive citizenship for the Transkei. Coupled with this is the stipulation that the whites cannot be citizens of the Transkei. Their aspirations must be realised in their own part of South Africa. This is the logical and consistent result of our policy of Separate Development. Constitutionally, according to this concept, every Bantu's citizenship will in the first place be established in his own homeland and every white's in white South Africa. The Republic of South Africa, of which the Transkei and the other Bantu homelands temporarily remain integral parts, is, according to international law, a sovereign state unit. A citizen of the Transkei and later also of the other self-governing Bantu states which will arise in South Africa, will still, until his state is *fully* independent for external purposes and according to international law, remain a citizen of South Africa, and as such enjoy protection.

The Territory

Clause 1 of the Bill makes it clear that the Transkei is a self-managing territory within the Republic of South Africa.

In clause 2 the territory which makes up the Transkei is defined. It is stated clearly that the Transkei consists of the Bantu territories of the 26 Transkeian districts which are mentioned in this clause. (See map, page 96)

Clause 3 provides that Bantu territories can be added to the Transkei, but only with the approval of the Transkeian Legislative Assembly. This clause thus gives a clear guarantee to the whites outside the Transkei, as well as to the Bantu of the Transkei, that no borders can be changed arbitrarily or in a one-sided manner or without the approval of chosen representatives of the people.

Flag, Anthem and Official Language

In clauses 4 to 6 provision is made for separate flag and anthem for the Transkei, and it also determines that Xhosa will be an official language of the territory. Provision is also made for the official languages of the Republic, and also for Sotho, to be used in official matters.

Citizenship

Clauses 7 and 8 of the Bill deal with citizenship.

1. In the first place a distinct citizenship for the Transkei is created.

2. All Xhosa-speaking Bantu in the Republic, and those in the Transkei, as well as those outside and also the Sotho-speaking Bantu of the Transkei and Bantu which are related to them, as well as other Bantu who were born in the Transkei or who for more than five years have legally been domiciled there, become citizens of the Transkei.

3. Transkeian citizens will enjoy and exercise all the citizenship rights and privileges which this Bill grants them such as, amongst others, the vote in the Transkei, and

will also be subject to the citizenship duties and responsibilities in the Transkei which this law places upon them.

4. Because they are actually citizens of a self-governing territory which is presently still for international purposes part of the Republic of South Africa, they will not be regarded or treated as foreigners in the Republic. They are thus placed on a different footing to the Bantu from outside the Republic.

The Cabinet

In clauses 9 to 22 provision is made for the executive branch of the Transkei to consist of a cabinet which initially comprises a Chief Minister and five other Ministers.

1. The cabinet is endowed with executive powers in all matters referred to it and the Legislative assembly is legally empowered in these matters;

2. The Chief Minister as well as the other Ministers are chosen by the Legislative Assembly (in secret ballot);

3. The period of office of the cabinet is the same as that of the Legislative Assembly—normally five years—but the cabinet or a member of the cabinet may be removed at the request of the Legislative Assembly.

The Legislative Assembly

Clauses 23 to 42 include the regulations in connection with the Legislative Assembly.

Clause 23 rules that the Legislative Assembly will consist of—

the Paramount Chiefs of the Transkei (there are 4); the 60 existing Chiefs, and 45 elected members.

It is clear that we are providing for a joint government by the traditional Bantu management authority and elected members who will be elected by the enfranchised citizens of the Transkei—the citizens in the Transkei and those outside.

Clause 26 rules that regional authority areas will be the constituencies for the election of the 45 members and each constituency will be able to elect a number of members in proportion to its registered voters. Also clauses 27, 28 and 29 include the qualification requirements for voters and members. Clause 30 rules that the period of office of the Legislative Assembly will be five years, unless the State President

A Polling officer registers a chief for the first general election in the new state of the Transkei.

A Transkeian tribesman in contemplative mood.

dissolves it earlier on the recommendation of the cabinet. Clauses 37, 38 and 39 deal with mechanics of legislation and additional powers.

Chieftainship and Lower Control Bodies

Clauses 43 to 47 rule:

1. That the duties, powers and function of chiefs as well as Bantu authorities (excluding the Territorial Authority) at present employed in the Transkei, will remain valid until such time as the empowered authority changes it;

2. The personal status of paramount chiefs be safeguarded;

3. Provision be made for the dissolving of the Transkeian Territorial Authority and the transfer of all the powers of this body and its possessions to the Transkeian Government.

Justice

In clauses 48 to 50 the following provisions are made with regard to courts in the Transkei:

(a) Existing lower courts, that is magisterial and Bantu Affairs Commissioners' Courts, can be transferred to the Transkeian Government and this Government will, where necessary, establish courts in accordance with the Magistrates' Court Act and the Bantu Administration Act, or, if it is so desired, accept legislation to establish its own courts.

(b) Provision is made in clause 50 for the establishment of a High Court for the Transkei. Sub-clause (3) stipulates that there is a right of appeal from this High Court to the Appeal Court.

Finance

Clause 51 of the Bill provides for the establishment of an autonomous Revenue Account for the Transkei into which all revenue must be paid. Clause 52 defines the revenue that will accrue to the Transkei. In short, this amounts to the Transkei receiving:

(i) All the personal taxes paid by Transkeian citizens; both within and outside the Transkei as well as such other taxes as may be imposed by the Transkeian Government itself;

(ii) All income taxes payable by Transkeian citizens and

private Bantu companies within the Transkei as well as estate duties payable in respect of the estates of Transkeian citizens who at the time of their decease had normally resided in the Transkei;

(iii) All administrative revenues, fines and funds arising from matters being administered by the Transkeian Government;

(iv) An annual amount payable from Consolidated Revenue Funds and based on the present expenditures of the Republican Government in the Transkei and

(v) Such an additional amount of money as may be voted annually by the South African Parliament.

Further, this portion of the Bill provides, inter alia, for—

(i) Parliamentary control over all expenditures, i.e. control by the Transkeian Legislative Assembly over all expenditures.

(ii) Compiling budgets and budgetary legislation;

(iii) The manner in which monies may be withdrawn—also by means of special warrants and

(iv) For the auditing of the Transkeian Revenue Account by the Controller and Auditor-General and for the application of our Treasury and Audit Act of 1956 until such time as the Transkei has made its own arrangements in this regard.

It is also important in regard to financial matters that we observe in general the principle that tax liability be linked with citizenship, i.e. a citizen should pay taxes for his own homelands and where he enjoys the franchise. Personal taxes of Xhosa citizens therefore accrue to the Transkei even when they live outside the Territory, and the taxes of whites in the Transkei accrue to the South African government.

Lands

Clause 59 of the Bill provides for the transfer to the Transkeian Government by proclamation of land and other public properties relating to matters over which the Transkeian Legislative Assembly exercises control, subject to such conditions as may be imposed.

Clause 60 chiefly relates to "white spot" villages in the Transkei and provides for their taking over by the Bantu.

Administration

As far as the transfer of administration and personnel

affairs are concerned, provision is made in broad outline in clauses 61 to 64 for the following, namely:

(i) Bantu officials at present working in the Transkei in departments or in connection with matters to be entrusted to the Transkei, will become officials of the Transkeian government as from the establishment of that government.

(ii) Such officials will, however, retain the pension benefits which they at present enjoy in our Public Service.

(iii) Since the Transkei at present does not have enough trained Bantu to fill all the posts in those departments which are to be transferred to its care, white officials will be put at the disposal of the Transkei to cope with these services.

(iv) These white officials will, however, remain in the service of the Government of the Republic and will also be paid by the Republic.

(v) These white officials will gradually be replaced by Bantu.

The First Schedule

The last and most important section of the Bill is the First Schedule wherein all the matters are incorporated over which the Transkei will obtain legal as well as administrative powers in terms of the provisions of the Bill.

So, for example, amongst others, the Transkei will control:

(i) Education in its entirety.

(ii) Agriculture, forestry and veterinary services.

(iii) Roads and works, except the interstate highways.

(iv) Labour and social services.

(v) Justice: courts and police services.

(vi) Lands, land control, deeds and survey services.

(vii) Estates, successions, births, deaths and marriages.

CONCRETE STEPS TO INDEPENDENCE

No state can function without the development of its human material as well as its natural resources. In the Transkei the policy has always been to help the underdeveloped Transkeians to help themselves with the knowledge that the white man must eventually withdraw from that area. But in South Africa, where the whims of colonialism affected both the rooted white nation and the Bantu, withdrawal has to be systematic if it is not going to degenerate into chaos. White South Africa has thus followed a policy of "internal decolonization" with respect to the Transkei. Only in this way, in this unique multi-national country, can viable nation states be born. That this approach of "live and let live" is working is borne out by achievements that speak more forcibly than the words of those who wish to sow confusion and dissent.

The Government devoted about $162 million to the physical development of the Bantu homelands during the five-year period 1961-66. This includes $26 million for the development of the Transkei. The estimated total amount for the Xhosa-speaking homelands is $47 million.

EDUCATION

The Transkei has made more progress in the educational field than any other Bantu territory in the Republic and is more advanced than most independent African states. As regards primary education there are schooling facilities for 85 per cent of all children in the school-going age group of seven to fourteen years.

The first school was opened as far back as 1800. Missionaries belonging to the various churches and mission societies were responsible for the first formal education of the Bantu.

The Wesleyan (Methodist) Church established a large number of mission stations which also provided educational facilities and it was in this manner that the following educational institutions came into being: Lamplough (Butterworth); Clarkebury (1830), Buntingville (1830), Shawbury, Palmerton, Emfundisweni (1865), Tsomo and Osborn (1850).

St. John's College, Umtata (Anglican Mission Society); Blythswood (Scottish Mission Society); Mvenyane, Cedarville (Moravian Mission Society) and Mariazell Institution (Roman Catholic Mission Society), had similar origins.

At a later stage the "Nederduitse Gereformeerde Kerk" (one of the "Dutch Reformed" churches) built schools in the Transkei, such as the Circira Teachers' Training School, Umtata, and the Arthur Tsengiwe Teachers' Training and Secondary School, Cala.

The missionaries were also the first persons to evolve a written script for the Bantu languages, and the Rev. J. W. Appleyard translated the Bible into Xhosa in 1859.

Government Interest

The Government first entered the field of Bantu education in 1854 when Sir George Grey, Governor of the Cape Colony, decided to subsidise mission schools for the vocational training of Bantu children, and for their training as interpreters, evangelists and teachers in the service of their own people.

In 1865 schools and institutions for Bantu were placed under the control of the Department of Education of the Cape Colony.

With the establishment of Union in 1910 primary and secondary education were entrusted to the various provincial

Top: The left wing of the vast Tembuland hospital in the Transkei. Center: Transkeian teacher at his class. The Transkeians are the most literate nation in all of black Africa. Bottom— Bantu blind being taught basket weaving at the Efata school.

authorities, and education in the Transkei thus became the responsibility of the Cape Provincial Administration. The mission societies continued, however, to be responsible for the instruction of Bantu children. The Government was responsible mainly for the financing of education.

In 1953 the Bantu Education Act (No. 47 of 1953) transferred the control of Bantu education from the Provincial Administration to the then Native Affairs Department of the Central Government, and in 1958 an independent Department of Bantu Education came into being.

Bantu Interest

One of the most important objects of the Bantu Education Act was to encourage the Bantu to play an active part in the management of their own schools. This made it necessary to alter the policy of supporting mission schools as well as the status of mission superintendents.

In 1954 the church bodies were given the option of either retaining control of their schools without any financial assistance or having the subsidy in respect of teachers' salaries, cost-of-living allowances and other allowances reduced to 75 per cent or transferring the control of their schools to the Department.

Various types of schools were established:

(a) Government Bantu schools, which include all schools for the children of State employees and are erected on State-owned land, and teachers' training schools.

(b) Bantu community schools.

(c) Aided farm, mine or factory schools which are erected on farm, factory or mine property for the children employees.

(d) Non-aided (private) schools.

The control of Bantu community schools was transferred to the Bantu school boards and committees established in terms of the Act. This system gave the Bantu parent a direct voice in the education of his child.

The total number of 252,784 school-going children represents approximately 70 per cent of all children of school-going age, higher than in most independent African states.

Children in the Lower Primary Schools receive instruction

in Xhosa (the mother tongue), Afrikaans, English, Arithmetic, Social Studies, Hygiene, Religious Instruction, Nature Study, Music and practical subjects such as Tree Planting and Soil Conservation, Needlework, Handicrafts, Arts and Crafts and Gardening.

The teaching profession is a career in which a large number of Bantu serve their own people: 4,358 Bantu are teaching at subsidised schools in the Transkei as against 235 teachers at private schools. Moreover, 54 white teachers are entrusted with the instruction of Bantu children in that area.

There are at present eight white inspectors, eight Bantu sub-inspectors and 29 Bantu supervisors in the Transkei.

Jongilizwe College

Since 1959 provision has been made for the training of sons of chiefs and headmen. This training is designed to equip the youths for their future calling and special attention is devoted to developing qualities of leadership, a sense of responsibility and administrative ability.

Vocational Training

There are at present five institutions providing vocational training for the Transkeians. Courses are offered in such subjects as masonry, carpentry, tailoring, etc.

Near Alice in the Ciskei is the University College of Fort Hare. Xhosa-speaking students continue their studies here and qualify in arts, science or commerce.

Special Instruction

The Efata school for blind and deaf Bantu children near Umtata helps to provide for the educational needs of such handicapped children. This school was established by the "Nederduits Gereformeerde" Bantu church of South Africa and subsidised by the Department of Bantu Education.

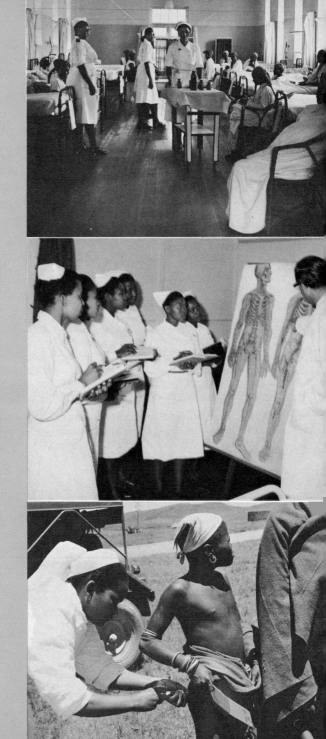

Nurses and patients in a Transkei hospital. Centre: Transkeian nurses attend an anatomy lecture at the Sir Herbert Elliott hospital in Umtata. Below: A young Transkeian is inoculated against polio (the Xhosa do not like to be scarified on the arms). Transkeian nurses and doctors administering the vaccine were successful in prevailing over superstitious beliefs, fostered by witchdoctors, against the value of inoculation.

The school's division for the blind was opened in 1958. The children are taught braille and, as far as is practicable, follow the normal school syllabus. They also receive tuition in handicrafts so as to assist them to earn their own living later.

The division for deaf children was opened in 1960. These children are taught to talk and to fend for themselves with a view to becoming socially effective individuals.

Health Services

As is the case in the rest of the Republic of South Africa, health services in the Transkei are decentralised. They are administered by the Department of Health, the Cape Provincial Administration, mission hospitals and clinics under the supervision of local authorities and Bantu authorities.

Three hospitals cater for infectious diseases, namely the Tembuland Tuberculosis Hospital near Umtata; Mkambati (Lusikisiki) and Mjanyana (Engcobo).

The Tembuland Hospital is the centre for the fight against tuberculosis in the Transkei. It is from here that four mobile X-ray units visit the various districts to make regular inspections of tuberculotics and their contacts. The whole of the X-ray division is managed by locally-trained Transkeians.

Mission hospitals play an important role in the Transkei and receive a subsidy from the Department in respect of infectious diseases. Tuberculotic patients are catered for by two S.A.N.T.A. (South African National Tuberculosis Association) settlements, one at Umtata and the other at Matatiele. The Transkei now has 15 hospitals containing 1,235 beds for persons suffering from infectious diseases. Approval has been obtained for the construction of a further seven mission hospitals for tuberculotics, and three of these are already being built.

There are 294 clinics in the Transkei of which 30 have been established and are being maintained by Bantu committees.

District surgeons are performing medical services for the Department on a part-time basis such as routine or mass inoculations against enteric fever, diphtheria and whooping cough, all of which are provided free of charge to the Bantu. These campaigns have achieved a great deal of success over the past few years thanks to a tactful approach and the willing co-operation of chiefs and headmen.

Provincial hospitals are found in the following Transkeian districts: Butterworth, Matatiele, Mount Fletcher and Um-

Pine trees stacked before transport to the timber factory at Vulindlela.

tata. Provincial and mission hospitals together contain a total of 2,980 general and 170 confinement beds for Transkeians.

AGRICULTURE

Climatically speaking, the Transkei is in a very favourable position and has a relatively high agricultural potential. In spite of this favourable climate the level of production is relatively low as the unscientific farming methods traditionally employed by the Bantu have greatly contributed to the deterioration of the soil.

The Bantu regard cattle as wealth and more often than not ignore quality in favour of quantity. They have tended to overstock and overgraze their land which has contributed to its destruction and erosion. Lack of judicious farming systems has also led to impoverishment of the soil.

Although planning has been undertaken in the Transkei for many years it is only since 1954 that positive steps have been taken to develop this region on a more scientific basis.

Any developmental programme that differs materially from the traditional system to which the Bantu are accustomed, has little chance of succeeding without the co-operation of the Bantu themselves. If it is accepted that Bantu farming methods must conform to sound principles and that land must be allocated to Bantu farmers in such a manner that they can become economically independent, it follows that many families will have to forfeit their land rights and settle in towns to find other means of livelihood. Attention is also being given to the establishment of industries which will create further employment for the non-farming Bantu population of the future.

Soil Conservation

Soil conservation works involve the application of all measures calculated to prevent the impoverishment of the soil and the reduction of its productivity. They include the construction of contour banks, grass-stripping, the establishment of watering-places for stock in all grazing camps so as to prevent the formation of paths to distant watering-points and the proper fencing-off of pastures so as to make the best use of the veld without harming it in any way.

Bantu traditions in regard to utilisation of land for agricultural purposes are so completely at variance with the practices on which scientific agriculture is based that the possibility of building up an independent and effective Bantu

farming community in the Transkei will depend on the extent to which the Bantu can be prevailed upon to accept scientific field husbandry practices. They have still to be convinced of the desirability of using good quality seed of the most suitable varieties and will have to pay more attention to the preparation and cultivation of the soil, the eradication of noxious weeds, fertilisation, etc., in order to obtain a higher level of productivity.

The failure of the Bantu to employ sound agronomic practices is reflected in the disappointing average yield of both maize and sorghum, the two most important staple food crops. Demonstration plots have proved that, with good agricultural practices and methods of cultivation, the yield can easily be increased.

In all planning projects it is always endeavoured to place as much land as possible under irrigation in order to ensure larger and more regular yields.

Fibre Cultivation

During the last few years a new project, namely the cultivation of fibre, was embarked upon in the Bantu areas as there is a great demand for it in the Republic of South Africa. The climate and soil of certain parts of the Bantu areas are suitable for the cultivation of fibre crops, which can be used in the place of jute for the manufacture of bags. (Jute is still imported.)

The Transkei, particularly those regions which lie between Lusikisiki and the coast, is one of the most promising parts of the country for the cultivation of *Phormium tenax* and that is why its cultivation is receiving special attention.

Fibre planting has been undertaken in the districts of Lusikisiki, Ngqeleni, Kentani and Butterworth.

Many Transkeians have already been employed to assist in the planting, cultivation and proper maintenance of the fibre plants as well as in cutting, decortication and pre-treatment for marketing purposes or for sale to factories manufacturing bags and other jute articles.

This new undertaking is creating new and increased interest in the future economic expansion of the Bantu homelands since it provides employment for the family as a whole. Moreover, it is helping to make the whole Republic of South Africa more self-sufficient in regard to the production of fibre.

Animal Husbandry

Overgrazing is one of the main causes of soil erosion and the general decline of the Bantu areas. Other important factors in this deterioration are the uneven distribution of livestock in the grazing areas and the difficulty of convincing the Bantu that the quality of their stock is more important than the quantity.

Bantu are encouraged to take part in co-operative dairy projects, 33 of which have already been established.

The agricultural section also organises agricultural shows in co-operation with the Bantu authorities. These shows are of great value and serve to acquaint the Bantu with the advantages of better farming methods.

Information

Although all these methods are employed to a greater or a lesser extent, experience has shown that personal contact is the most successful of all, particularly when it is through the medium of Bantu extension officers who enjoy the confidence of the farmers.

Hitherto this type of medium has not been fully exploited as most of the available manpower has been used for planning.

Further information is disseminated by means of radio talks on agricultural matters and the regular publication of such articles in the Transkeian Government's agricultural magazine, "Umcebisi Womlini Numfuyi."

Schools are emphasising the vital importance of soil conservation and scientific agricultural methods, helping to create an awareness of the need for better farming methods amongst the youth of the Transkei.

The Tsolo Agricultural School

The Tsolo Agricultural school was established in 1913 and now falls under the control of the Transkeian Authority. The school farm is also situated near Tsolo and covers an area of 3,000 acres.

There are facilities for the training of 80 students every year. In addition to their theoretical training the students receive practical training in animal husbandry, agriculture, fish breeding and all matters pertaining to farming in the Transkei. They are also taught the basic requirements for the maintenance of farming machinery and implements.

After completion of the initial 18 months' course students may enroll for a further course designed to qualify them as assistant stock inspectors as well as for a diploma course.

This school may rightly be regarded as the central source from which the Xhosa youth and farming population can derive their agricultural knowledge and guidance.

Fisheries

The fishing industry is still in its infancy and has not developed much beyond the experimental stage.

Recognising the importance of fish in the daily diet of the Bantu, the Transkeian Government has established an experimental fishery station at the Tsolo Agricultural School. It is the ultimate aim to stock all dams built near new towns.

Forestry

Owing to its high annual rainfall the Transkei is particularly suitable for the successful commercial planting of trees; indeed the Tomlinson Commission for the Socio-Economic Development of the Bantu areas recommended the afforestation of 141,000 acres.

The indigenous forests of the Territories have been denuded by the Bantu in search of firewood and poles. They use young trees for house building purposes, and this has resulted in a reduction in the natural increase of the forests.

During the last decade of the 19th century a start was made in demarcating existing forests and in establishing plantations to provide the Transkeians with timber for use as firewood and roofing material. In 1936, for instance, 56 plantations had been planted for this purpose over an area of 7,000 acres. The total area under plantations in that year was approximately 15,000 acres.

Reserved indigenous forests now cover an area of 160,431 acres and are patrolled by 95 Bantu forest rangers. The following indigenous trees are found in these forests: Yellowwood, Black Stinkwood, Camdeboo Stinkwood, Black Ironwood, White Ironwood, Lemonwood, Sneezewood, Cabbagewood, Assegaaiwood, Red Pear, Cape Boxwood, Cape Mahogany, Nzimbete, Cape Ebony, Hard Pear, Terblanche, Cape Chestnut. Plantations consist mainly of varieties of pines as well as eucalyptus and wattles.

Mr. K. Matanzima and the late Mr. Dag Hammarskjöld a few weeks before Mr. Hammarskjöld's death in Zambia in an air crash. The former Secretary General of the U.N. paid a visit to South Africa in 1961. Mr. Hammarskjöld made an extensive tour through the Transkei and had the opportunity to consult with South Africans of all shades of opinion.

Chapter V

Matanzima—Leader of the Xhosa State

C HIEF KAIZER MATANZIMA became the Chief Minister of the Transkei, the first of South Africa's Bantu homelands to achieve internal self-government. He was elected by 54 votes to 49 by the new Legislative Assembly of the Transkei that was constituted after the election of November 20, 1963.

His chief rival was Paramount Chief Victor Poto.

Mr. Kaizer D. Matanzima is a man of great ability and is today regarded as one of the most promising leaders in southern Africa. As a natural-born leader he is dedicated to fight Communism and to help his people towards a better way of life. He founded the first secondary school in the district of Xalanga, encouraged the establishment of clinics and co-operated fully with missionaries and the authorities. Today, several additional schools are being built in his district as result of his trail-blazing activities.

Born in 1915, son of a Paramount Chief, the young man received his schooling at the Lovedale Missionary Institution where he was honoured with the Andrew Smith Award.

Chief Matanzima's father, the late Chief Mhlobo Mvuzo Matanzima Mtirara who reigned over Emigrant Tembuland, died in 1932 and his uncle, Daluble Matanzima, was appointed Regent to act during Matanzima's minority. His tribe admired and respected his qualities and finally decided to

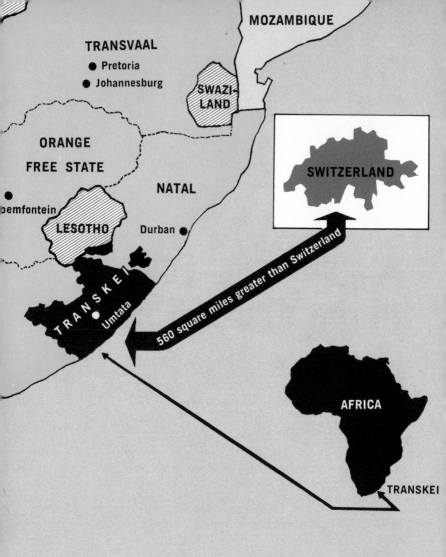

Countries	Area in square miles	Population
TOGO	21,893	1,440,000
BURUNDI	10,747	2,234,141
RUANDA	10,069	2,694,749
ISRAEL	7,992	2,170,082
LESOTHO	11,716	727,000
TRANSKEI	16,500	3,044,000

send him to Fort Hare University. In 1939 he obtained the Degree of Bachelor of Arts, having majored in Roman Law and Political Science. Shortly after graduation he was installed as Chief of the Ama-Hala Clan of the Tembu and immediately started to make representations to the South African Government to recognize his hereditary status as Chief of the Emigrant Tembu.

During his term of office Chief Matanzima took articles of clerkship for the attorney's admission examination. He qualified in 1948 and won the Cape of Good Hope Law Society Award for his outstanding performance.

While still studying to become a lawyer he became a member of the United Transkeian Authorities General Council which was transformed in 1956 to the Transkeian Territorial Authority. He served as a member of the Recess Committee which drafted the Transkeian Territorial Bantu Authorities Proclamation which subsequently became law. By the provisions of this law he automatically became permanent head of the Emigrant Tembuland Regional Authority and received a seat in the Transkeian Territorial Authority and its Executive Committee.

In 1958 Chief Matanzima was officially recognized as Regional Chief of the Emigrant Tembuland and in 1961 the Transkeian Territorial Authority elected him as successor to Paramount Chief Botha Sigcau as chairman of this parliamentary governing body for the Xhosa-speaking peoples. In his first address he called for "patience, determination and statesmanship in dealing with the affairs of the people."

"Communism," he said, "is threatening the existence of all forms of democratic institutions."

On the subject of constitutional development he said: "Self-government has now become our resolved policy and there is no turning aside from the road we have taken."

Chief Matanzima supports the concept of Separate Development for South Africa's peoples, in terms of which the Bantu are gradually assuming control of their own affairs in their territories.

After the Chief Minister had been chosen, the Legislative Assembly met for a second time to elect the five cabinet ministers who assumed, with the Chief Minister, executive responsibility for the affairs of the Transkei. The Chief Minister is also Minister of Finance, and the other five ministers head the departments of agriculture and forestry, interior, education, justice, and roads and works.

Shortly before the opening of the Legislative Assembly, Mr. K.
Matanzima, the Chief Minister of the new State led a motor-
cade out of Umtata, the capital city to welcome Mr. C. R.
Swart, South Africa's State President to the new state. Here
Mr. Swart (centre) is being introduced to Mr. Matanzima by
South Africa's government representative in the Transkei,
Commissioner-General J. Abraham.

CHIEF MINISTER MATANZIMA'S
STATEMENT OF POLICY – JUNE 1966

During the past two years we of the Xhosa nation have had our first experience of self-government under the constitution adopted at the end of 1963 which gave us our own 109-member Legislature, our own Cabinet of Ministers chosen by this Legislative Assembly and our own Civil Service.

At its latest session the Assembly decided to present the design for our own flag to the people. Soon we hope to see this new symbol of our statehood in the Transkei—homeland of South Africa's Xhosa people—flying over an area larger than Massachusetts, Connecticut, Rhode Island and Delaware combined.

We have achieved all this by following the path of constitutional and evolutionary development and not the road of revolution that has led to so much turmoil, economic chaos and bloodshed elsewhere.

Controversy

We have achieved our aims within the framework of the Republic of South Africa's policy of separate development—a policy which has often been the subject of violent controversy.

Why is it that I, a black man and a Xhosa nationalist should endorse a policy which many well-meaning people in the United States criticize and condemn? Why is it that I urge the people of the Transkei to seek their political destiny in being a separate nation?

The fact of the matter is that South Africa is inhabited not simply by blacks and whites or by a black nation and a white nation. South Africa is inhabited by a white nation of European origin and by a number of markedly different black nations as different from each other in terms of customs, language and culture as the nations of Africa. Surely it is obvious that such a multi-national complex calls for differential treatment especially since each nation more or less settled its part of South Africa by right of first occupation.

It is my contention that representation for the twelve million Bantu in South Africa, or even just the Xhosa in a predominantly white Parliament, is doomed to failure. It would simply create endless conflict in our heterogeneous community and would bedevil the peaceful progress of all peoples and the prosperity of the country as a whole. It would not be progressive but retrograde.

Members of the Transkeian Legislative Assembly taking the oath of allegiance to their new state.

Democracy is one of the cornerstones of the political structure of
the new State. This picture shows
the members of the Transkei Oppo-
sition. Both government and oppo-
sition parties boast some of the
most learned men in Africa.

The State President of the Republic
of South Africa and the State of the
Transkei, Charles R. Swart, signs
into law the first Act passed by the
Transkeian Legislative Assembly.
The Act legalized the spending of millions of dollars (some of it South African
aid) for development in the new state. The new Transkei State, homeland of the
Xhosa nation, is on the way to full independence. It is hoped that the coopera-
tion between the Bantu Transkei and White Republic of South Africa will evolve
into a Commonwealth relationship crystalizing the general future pattern for
South Africa's policy of creative withdrawal from other Bantu areas within
South Africa. The constitutional forms of the Transkei are a blend of Western
democracy and traditional Xhosa forms of government.

101

Chief Minister Kaizer D. Matanzima.

Reject Amalgamation

Such a step would be a denial of the autonomy to which my people as a nation are entitled and likewise would deny the right of self-determination to all the other Bantu nations in South Africa. We do not wish to see our distinctive identity dissolved into a nondescript and uncertain conglomerate lacking a personality or culture of its own.

The Bantu peoples of South Africa, as I am sure is also the case in other parts of Africa, are proud of their heritage. They do not automatically regard it as an unblemished and unmixed blessing to be required to exchange their national and cultural possessions for those, for instance, of a European society.

We do not expect of the white man to sacrifice the national and cultural attributes which he holds dear.

The Transkei today has its own government, its own civil service, its own system of taxation. We can enjoy the fruits of our own victories or suffer the bitterness of our own defeats depending upon ourselves. This has been made possible by the same white government which has so often been accused of being dedicated to withholding from the black man the opportunity of advancement and self-determination.

There are, in my opinion, two roads leading to freedom— one peacefully, the other by revolution. The people who oppose the attainment of self-government under the existing Transkeian Constitution are the protagonists of the revolutionary approach.

Revolution

White South Africa is one hundred per cent agreed on the maintenance of white control of the white Parliament. It is my conviction that only their defeat on the battlefield will divest them of this resolution.

Will those people who oppose the peaceful road taken by the Transkei openly advocate a revolution?

The Transkei people, with the exception of the gullible ones who are easily misled, will not be duped into a situation which will ruin their country.

The whites who advocate a multi-racial parliament for the Transkei are not sincere. They know that if their ideas are accepted by the Bantu, whites will always control the affairs of the Transkei under the old slogan that "time is not ripe."

We, therefore, solidly stand by the Constitution of the Transkei and will under its provision ask at the appropriate time that greater powers and more comprehensive duties in respect of Transkeian matters be handed over to us so that we can develop towards complete autonomy.

We will preserve the land, improve our livestock and improve agricultural production by introducing scientific and progressive farming methods and modern planning. We will endeavour by all possible means to promote and encourage the economic and industrial development of the Transkei and the exploitation of its natural resources.

We will develop a sound and progressive educational system for the Transkei under the guidance of educational experts and will give particular attention to technical, industrial, commercial and vocational training and will foster study in the scientific, engineering, and allied fields.

Development Projects

We will preserve the traditional system of chieftainship in the Transkei and will build on our cultural heritage and traditions, taking from Western civilization and democracy that which we can best adapt to our way of life.

We will do our utmost to secure a state in the Transkei founded on law and order—a state that recognizes the dignity of the individual and which will ensure equal justice for all.

We re-affirm our friendship for the whites living in the Transkei and acknowledge our great indebtedness towards our administrators, traders and missionaries. However, we also stand for the gradual withdrawal of the whites from the Transkei so that this territory can become our own exclusive homeland. Yet our policy is and remains one of intimate friendship with our mother country, the Republic of South Africa.

The different parts of South Africa are interdependent and our future is tied up with that of greater South Africa.

One can foresee that eventually South Africa will embrace a number of fully Bantu-governed states linked with the white Republic of South Africa in cooperative association.

Chapter VI

South Africa Prospers

Address to The Executives' Club of Chicago by H. L. T. Taswell, South African Ambassador to the United States of America, Friday, 4th March, 1966.

RECENTLY a certain millionaire revealed that his personal fortune amounted to about $48 million. He likes to work on a cash basis, and put his "petty cash" resources at $5.6 million. In preparation for a big deal in properties, he had this "petty cash" counted out in bills. It took twenty assistants two days to complete the task.

This millionaire happens to be a black man living in the Republic of South Africa or, to be more precise, in the territory of the Transkei, the centuries-old home of the Xhosa people in the Republic.

The Transkei already has its own all-black Legislature, made up partly of traditional leaders and partly of members elected on a one-man-one-vote basis. Executive authority is vested in an all-black Cabinet. The territory has its own national anthem, its own official language and is currently deciding on the final design of its own flag. The territory's constitution, providing for self-government, came into effect two years ago. Of the 2,478 posts in its civil service, 1,900 were filled by black people. Within the next two or three years, all the posts should be filled by black people.

The biggest hospital on the continent of Africa treats on an average 2,000 in-patients and 2,000 out-patients *every single day of the year*. It performs 1,800 operations each month, and serves over 10,000 meals every twenty-four hours.

H. L. T. Taswell,
South African Ambassador to the United States

This hospital happens to be in the Republic of South Africa at Baragwanath, near Johannesburg, and it caters almost exclusively to black people.

In 1965, over 6,500 non-white undergraduates studied at South African universities. Among the Bantu alone in the Republic, there are already over 2,800 university graduates. In sixteen years, South African universities produced more black graduates than nine other countries on the African continent, with a population of seventy million, succeeded in doing in fifty years.

In other parts of independent Africa, the number of children at school, in the age group of 7-12, varies from 49 per cent, down to 5 per cent. In our country, it is 83 per cent among the Bantu alone and it is rising steadily. Today, virtually every black child in South Africa is within walking distance of a primary school.

No Foreign Aid

This year it is expected that American foreign aid to Africa will amount to about $205 million.

Not one cent of this will go to South Africa. We have never asked for or accepted foreign aid.

South Africa is one of only three countries in the world which have paid all their war debts.

Latest statistics indicate that American exports to South Africa in 1965 reached a record figure of about $438 million. Our exports to you were about $225 million, giving you a very favorable balance of trade.

Between 30 and 40 per cent of all American exports to the continent of Africa go to the Republic of South Africa.

Only thirteen other countries in the whole world purchase more from you than we do.

Your investments in our country are valued at between $489 million and $650 million. On these you obtain a very substantial return.

Total American and foreign investment in South Africa is equal to that on the rest of the African continent put together. People have not invested in our country for sentimental reasons. They have invested because of the soundness of our economy, because of the stability of our country and because we have given ample proof that we believe in the principles of free enterprise.

Our industrial, mining, agricultural and economic production has been prodigious. Annual gold production has reached a record level of over $1 billion. Between 1945 and 1964 industrial production increased six-fold. Our exports and imports last year reached new record levels.

Domestic capital formation has reached the point where we can, if necessary, maintain a reasonable rate of growth by financing developments solely from our own resources.

Our railroads carry as much freight as those on the rest of the continent put together. Latest figures show that we produce over seven times as much steel as the whole of the rest of Africa combined, ten times as much coal and over twice as much electricity.

About half of the telephones and automobiles in Africa are in our Republic. As a matter of interest, an independent survey showed that there is one car for every thirteen persons in South Africa. Only six other countries in the world show better figures for car ownership than that.

Skills have greatly improved in our country. From a technical point of view, the number of things which we cannot ourselves produce, is steadily diminishing. In common with the United States and Russia, we were one of the first three countries to make synthetic diamonds.

With only 6 per cent of Africa's population, we generate 20 per cent of the continent's total geographic income.

Prosperity Benefits All

All sections of our population benefit from our prosperity. That holds good for our Whites, whose ancestors came to South Africa over three hundred years ago and settled areas which were virtually unoccupied; it also holds good for our Coloured people, for our Indians, and for our Bantu or black national groups.

These various Bantu national groups, each one with its own language, customs and traditions, migrated from Central Africa at about the same time as whites settled at the Cape. The black national groups occupied other parts of the country.

Our very close association, over a long period of time, with all the various groups constituting our population has given us a keen insight into their customs, traditions and general way of life. It has brought to light the sharp contrasts between them and shown the frictions which can steadily arise when the differences are ignored.

Our aim is to improve relations between the various racial groups. We are against domination of any one race by another.

With this in mind, we are working in the direction of a commonwealth or common market, based on political independence and economic inter-dependence. Within this framework we see the formation ultimately of separate states for the whites and for the black, or Bantu, national groups and the development of the greatest degree of governmental autonomy for the Coloured people and for the Indians. We also see the creation of a consultative body in which leaders may meet on a basis of equality to consider matters of common interest and ways of removing possible friction.

The Transkei, to which I referred earlier, is one striking example of the positive progress we are making in this direction.

Such have been the achievements in our country that nowhere in independent Africa do people, regardless of their race or color, have as high a general standard of living, education or health as they do in South Africa.

Rhodesia

Forming part of Africa as we do, we in South Africa watch with keen interest the developments taking place in various parts of that continent.

We are frequently asked what our attitude is to events in Rhodesia, our immediate neighbor to the North, which declared its independence from Britain on 11th November, 1965.

As our Prime Minister recently pointed out, our basic policy is one of non-intervention in this domestic confrontation between Britain and Rhodesia. We deprecate the intervention of others.

The question which many people ask is whether the actions being taken against Rhodesia might not bring about a collapse of order and economic development and precipitate the very confusion which it is said the actions are designed to avoid. What sorely tried Africa needs is not further confusion but the maintenance of order, stability and peaceful development.

We in South Africa continue regular relations with both Britain and Rhodesia. We do not support or participate in any form of boycott, nor are we yielding to any pressure to do so.

We have, over a long period of years, maintained and promoted the closest of relations with Rhodesia. Our bonds of friendship and our economic ties have grown.

It is our aim to maintain ties of friendship with all neighboring countries, whether white or black. We are anxious to expand our trade with them, to improve our relations with them, to assist and cooperate with them in any way we can.

Ugly Realities

Much has been happening on the African continent of late to cause concern.

One government after another has been toppled—five alone by military take-over during the last four months.

Sad to relate, these events have frequently been accompanied by violence, bloodshed, a heavy toll of life, murder and even assassination. Some countries on which great hopes had been placed as models of stability and democracy, have crumbled. Developments have occurred which have unfortunately made a mockery of the Western concepts of majority rule and one-man-one-vote.

But what does not make the headlines is the untold human suffering, the hunger and disease that goes with all this, while leaders vie for position and try to undermine other countries.

There are many ugly realities in Africa from which people wish to hedge away. Collapsing economies, instability, falling standards of living, of education and of health have unfortunately characterized so many parts of Africa in recent years, following the rapid transition to independence.

Added to this there have been serious border clashes and other disorders. Tribal warfare in one country alone resulted in the slaughter of an estimated 8,000 men, women and children. A revolt in another country caused loss of life estimated at 40,000. Barbarous atrocities included the savage beating to death or shooting of people whose only apparent crime was that they could read and write.

We in South Africa have so often been told that we are wrong in what we are doing and that we must conform to the pattern in Africa. We in the Republic do not claim to be perfect, but Africa has certainly furnished us with some striking examples of just how not to run our affairs.

Two decades ago, there were only four independent states on the African continent. Early last year, the number rose to thirty-seven. We in South Africa have much sympathy and understanding for the peoples of Africa. We can readily appreciate their desire for independence. We, after all, strove for many years to obtain our own.

Many of the ills from which independent Africa is suffering can be traced to the attempts to impose a Western form of government on people which is not only foreign to their nature but one, in the arts of which, they have received very little training. Far too little value has been attached to the basic social structure on which so much of Africa has operated in the past and on which it will, no doubt, continue to operate for years to come. Attempts to destroy it—and there are many in progress—take away the very mainstay of African community life and create a dangerous void which promotes insecurity and instability.

Enemies of the West are profiting from instability in Africa and from the fact that African countries hold about one third of the total votes at the United Nations—this notwithstanding the fact that they contribute just over 2 per cent of the U.N. budget.

Red China is now represented in about seventeen countries in Africa. Roughly one third of all Peking's diplomatic missions throughout the world are in Africa. When the issue of Communist China's membership arose at the United Nations recently, the voting was 47-47. Of the African countries, eighteen voted in favor of seating Peking and seven abstained. South Africa took the same position as the United States and voted against admission.

Problems in Africa will not be solved by emotional hysteria or by the incessant repetition of hollow slogans and platitudes. Nor will the lasting friendship of the black man be won by undermining the white man in Africa as is still believed in certain quarters.

Proud of our Achievements

We are proud of our achievements in South Africa. Each day takes us a further step forward on our path of positive progress. Our aim is to allow all groups to preserve their own way of life and to prosper to the maximum of their ability without undermining one another.

To-day, nearly one million foreign Africans work in our country. One of our greatest problems is presented by the thousands of others who constantly cross our borders illegally in order to seek the benefits of life which our country has to offer.

We have great confidence in our future. We are jealous of our sovereignty and highly resentful of attempts to interfere in our internal affairs.

What we have built up during the last three hundred years is something which we are ready to defend with all the forces at our disposal.

In spite of the fact that some people in influential positions in your country at times make most uncomplimentary remarks about us, we remain friendly and well disposed towards the United States. American satellite and missile tracking stations in our country receive the fullest assistance from our Government. We do not nationalize American industries, nor do we defile the American flag.

2 6 9 3   5 7 9